Paulie's

"Paulie's is a staple of Montrose and exemplifies consistency and quality. It's the neighborhood spot that's a go-to for so many people that live and work in Montrose, myself included."

—**CHEF CHRIS SHEPHERD,** Underbelly and One Fifth

"Paul Petronella is like a post office rubber band. He is super useful, malleable to purpose, a classic in work ethic, and with some coaxing, can be turned into a musical instrument."

—**BRAD MOORE,** Grand Prize Bar, Honeymoon, and Bad News Bar

"Paul is obviously a hard worker and thinker. He took ownership of the OKRA kitchen when he didn't have to, which really shows his pride and joy in the industry itself. He made great decisions and included all of us. When he saw things weren't working, he changed them. I've been really impressed with his restaurant acumen."

—**CHEF RYAN PERA,** Agricole Hospitality

"Paul was instrumental when we established our coffee roasting company, Greenway Coffee Company. He was a day-one supporter and was our first official wholesale account. His support and dedication to local, quality-focused businesses is unparalleled in the city."

—**DAVID BUEHRER,** Blacksmith Coffee, Greenway Coffee, and Morningstar Coffee

"Paul, through Camerata, has created a space where I choose to have my important brainstorming sessions for new promotional ideas. The environment provides a rich background for creative inspiration and discussion through its high-level design, the amazing selections, the knowledgeable staff, and the clientele it attracts. There have been many nights when I have encountered individuals whose stories further inspired me. Other nights, I know that I can visit alone and be engaged by inspirational conversations from the staff or an interesting stranger, passing through Houston, who has discovered this gem. I'm grateful for Paul providing such an amazing oasis."

—**ANDRE SAM-SIN,** DJ Sun

"I take my close friends to Paulie's on a weekday date night—best eggplant parm I've ever had, and I love eggplant parm. We always leave feeling nourished."

—**KAREN MAN,** Oxheart

"The way I first met Paul speaks very much to who he is as a person. We had a mutual friend who suffered a head injury in a scooter accident. Of course, like many in the restaurant and bar industry, she had no insurance and needed major surgery for a terrible head injury. David Buehrer of Greenway Coffee and I planned a big fundraising event, and Paul stepped up immediately to host it. It was on a Sunday, when Paulie's is normally closed. The fundraiser took up the entire restaurant and parking lot. Thanks to vast community support, we were able to raise thousands in emergency funds for the victim. It wouldn't have been possible without Paul. That's just the kind of guy Paul is. When there's someone in Houston's restaurant and bar community in need, he's usually one of the first to step up and help out. The fact that he and his staff run a comfortable neighborhood Italian restaurant with killer pasta dishes and one of the best wine bars in Houston—well, that's just a bonus."

—**PHAEDRA COOK,** freelance food writer

Paulie's

PAUL PETRONELLA

Paulie's

CLASSIC ITALIAN COOKING *in the*

HEART *of* HOUSTON'S MONTROSE DISTRICT

GREENLEAF
BOOK GROUP PRESS

Published by Greenleaf Book Group Press
Austin, Texas
www.gbgpress.com

Distributed by Greenleaf Book Group

For ordering information or special discounts for bulk purchases, please contact
Greenleaf Book Group at PO Box 91869, Austin, TX 78709, 512.891.6100.

Design and composition by Greenleaf Book Group
Cover design by Greenleaf Book Group
Cover illustration by Matt Manalo
Photography and styling by Debora Smail
Other image credits: Family Tree (6-7) image credit: Monica Fuentes; Italy illustration (36)
photo credit: Hayley Riccio; Frame image (36) image credit: ©shutterstock.com/
Thawornnurak; Butera's logo (58) image credit: Matt Manalo;
Tiffany's ad photo (170) image credit: Fulton Davenport.

Cataloging-in-Publication data is available.

Print ISBN: 978-1-62634-468-6
ebook ISBN: 978-1-62634-505-8

Part of the Tree Neutral® program, which offsets the number of trees consumed in
the production and printing of this book by taking proactive steps, such as planting
trees in direct proportion to the number of trees used: www.treeneutral.com

Printed in China on acid-free paper

18 19 20 21 22 23   10 9 8 7 6 5 4 3 2

First Edition

I would like to dedicate this book to the founders of Paulie's, Bernard and Kathy Petronella, and also to the entire Paulie's family, past and present, including but definitely not limited to Maria, Edwin, Abraham, Beatriz, Delmer, Tony, Jesus, Lucero, Norma, Marcella, Josue, Edgar, Tino, Matt Z, Becca, Jenna, Haley, Carlo, Jon, Dean, Dan, Kristina, Audrey, Vasili, Lindsey M . . .

CONTENTS

Acknowledgments

Thank you to everyone who helped me through the process of bringing this book to life, including everyone at Greenleaf Book Group, Debora Smail, with her creativity and amazing camera work, and all those I pressured into reading my manuscript. Writing a book is a complicated process; there is no way this would be possible without professionals like you.

Introduction

Thank you for selecting this book full of stories, food, and photos. It follows my and my family's journey through the process of opening Paulie's to our current-day success. It also provides insight into the restaurant business and the daily grind that is the hospitality industry.

This book is unique in its story and layout. Most cookbooks arrange similar dishes together—entrees, meat, poultry, desserts, and so on. This is a book about story first, a recipe book second. As you read, you will notice the recipes fit into the story line. If you're looking for a particular recipe, flip back to the index, and it'll take you right to it.

Although this book is intended to celebrate twenty years of Paulie's success with recipes and photos, it also includes authentic Italian dishes from either my childhood or my time in Italy. When considering which recipes to include, I wanted to share dishes that could be easily recreated at home. There are items on the Paulie's menu that would be difficult to recreate without commercial equipment or sourced ingredients. I own cookbooks from all over the world. I know how it feels to come across a recipe that is impossible to duplicate at home, and I cook for a living! Keep practicing and cooking through each recipe until you are happy with it. Cooking is about finding your own style and voice. If you prefer different ingredients or herbs, please find your own favorite composition. Enjoy our story and our food in your kitchen!

Charles Petronella, Nash D'Amico, Damian Mandola and Phillip Barletta at Damian's in Huntsville, TX

CHAPTER 1

Under the Feet of Greatness

For as long as I can remember, my family has been in the restaurant business. In the late 1970s, my uncle Charles teamed up with his cousins Nash D'Amico and Damian Mandola to open their own place. This was D'Amico's, located on Westheimer Road, near Kirby Drive, in my hometown of Houston, Texas. As I remember it, D'Amico's was a bit progressive for Houston at that time. It was definitely one of Houston's fanciest spots for Italian food.

My father, Bernard, my aunt Mary, my uncle Frank, and my uncle Ronald, along with a gaggle of cousins, all worked at D'Amico's. When I was only about four years old and about three feet tall, I was already running around the kitchen, weaving in and out of line cooks, trying to stay out of the way, yet hoping to be in the action. I spent more time ducking under counters and dodging quick-moving kitchen staff than I ever did on a playground. Maybe that's why I prefer to be in the kitchen.

One of my favorite memories of D'Amico's is of one-time Los Angeles Dodgers manager Tommy Lasorda. He visited the restaurant whenever the Dodgers were playing the Astros. I was a huge baseball nut growing up, and I'd always ask if he was coming in. One day, a package arrived at the door of our home from Tommy addressed to my father. It was a box full of autographed photos of the 1981 World Champion LA Dodgers. I held on to that box all the way to early adulthood; I wish I could tell you where it is now.

At D'Amico's, and later at my uncle Charles's restaurant, Rocco's, I spent nights sleeping in the restaurant office or snuggled up to the bar with a Cherry Coke and a mouthful of cocktail vegetables. Even at an early age, I was being conditioned to the irregular restaurant schedule. I was often covered with the scents of garlic, tomato sauce, and smoke, and I grew to love those smells. They represent my childhood. I once enjoyed a wine at the Terroir wine bar in New York that tasted and smelled exactly like canned pizza sauce. It was incredibly nostalgic. I have been looking for that bottle ever since.

At D'Amico's, we made all of the classic Italian-American sauces and dishes that I still love, such as clam sauce, veal parmigiana, picatta, scampi, vodka sauce, lobster ravioli, saltimbocca, and puttanesca. These foods have so much flavor, usually contributed to by heavy doses of garlic and love. My favorites were always a simple scampi with fettuccini, pasta with red sauce, and lobster ravioli.

As a small child, a busy restaurant was always exciting. There was always such contrast among the kitchen, where there was organized yelling between the cooks; the dining room, where the ambiance and the people were calm and sophisticated; and the bar, where most of the patrons were inebriated but always interested in knowing who the roaming child was.

The restaurant employees worked hard and played hard, and they spent money just as fast as they made it. It was a fast-paced, rock-star lifestyle. At D'Amico's, the Petronellas tried out for the game show *Family Feud*. They made the cut and actually won their episode in a wild upset, the other family having led for most of the episode. The show was filmed in Los Angeles, and they left all of their winnings there that night.

I was intrigued by tableside preparations at D'Amico's, such as Caesar salad and spaghetti carbonara, and the mysterious fried ice cream. If I had to compare D'Amico's to a restaurant today, it would be Carbone, in New York City. The food is classic and well executed, and the service is top-notch. Carbone pays respect to the old-school Italian-American restaurants from my childhood.

◀ Petronella and Torregrossa Family dining at D'Amicos circa 1982.

A HOUSTON CULINARY

Tony Lamonte — Josephine Lamonte

Vi M

Charles Pizzitola — Pauline Pizzitola

Maggie M. Lamonte — Thomas Lamonte

Lena Lamonte — Joseph Mandola

F Ma

Nash Frank D'Amico — Rosalie Pizzitola

Frank Paul Petronella — Delia Mary Petronella

Mary Lamonte — Anthony Lamonte

Nash Frank D'Amico Jr.

6,8

Kathy Petronella

14

Bernard Petronella

14

Louann Lamonte

Brina Rose D'Amico

6

Paul Petronella

14

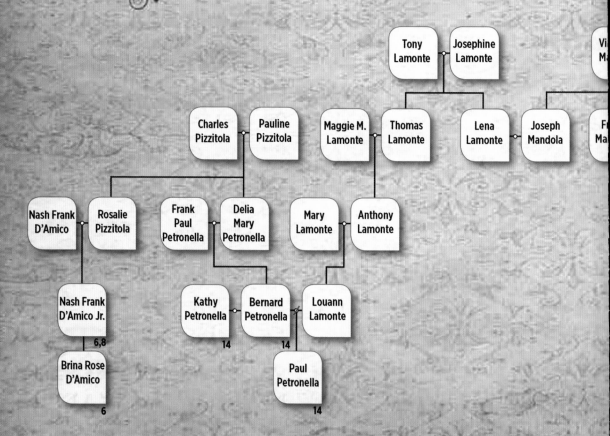

The information in this family history, which we gathered from interviews and ancestry.com, is not intended to be comprehensive. For the sake of clarity, we've included only those mentioned in the story or necessary to link one individual to another.
–○–: Married   –⚬–: Divorced

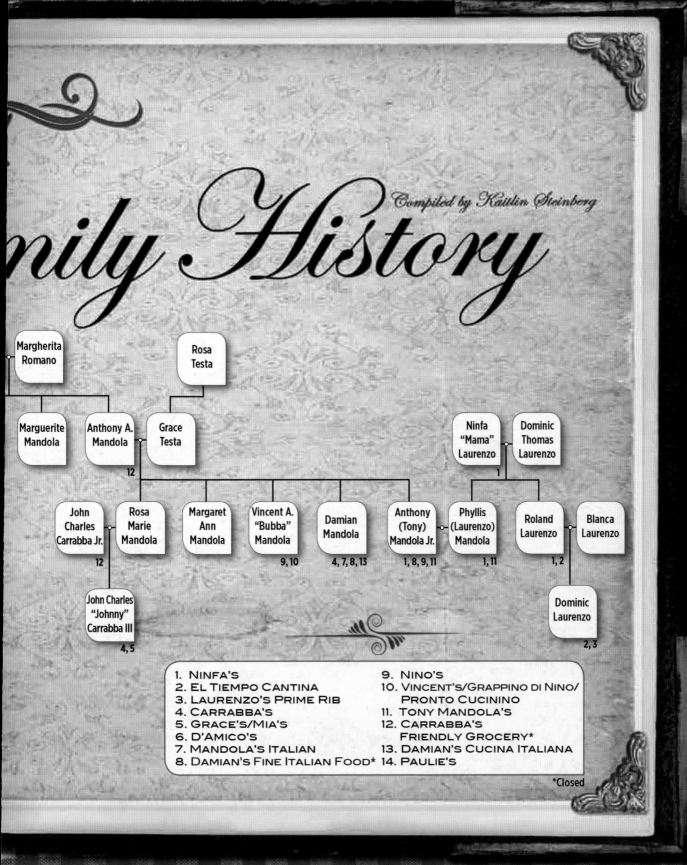

Family History

Compiled by Kaitlin Steinberg

Margherita Romano

Rosa Testa

Marguerite Mandola

Anthony A. Mandola

Grace Testa
12

Ninfa "Mama" Laurenzo

Dominic Thomas Laurenzo
1

John Charles Carrabba Jr.
12

Rosa Marie Mandola

Margaret Ann Mandola

Vincent A. "Bubba" Mandola
9, 10

Damian Mandola
4, 7, 8, 13

Anthony (Tony) Mandola Jr.
1, 8, 9, 11

Phyllis (Laurenzo) Mandola
1, 11

Roland Laurenzo
1, 2

Blanca Laurenzo

John Charles "Johnny" Carrabba III
4, 5

Dominic Laurenzo
2, 3

1. NINFA'S
2. EL TIEMPO CANTINA
3. LAURENZO'S PRIME RIB
4. CARRABBA'S
5. GRACE'S/MIA'S
6. D'AMICO'S
7. MANDOLA'S ITALIAN
8. DAMIAN'S FINE ITALIAN FOOD*
9. NINO'S
10. VINCENT'S/GRAPPINO DI NINO/ PRONTO CUCININO
11. TONY MANDOLA'S
12. CARRABBA'S FRIENDLY GROCERY*
13. DAMIAN'S CUCINA ITALIANA
14. PAULIE'S

*Closed

Fettuccini Scampi

In Italy, the term *scampi* usually refers to langoustines, prawns, or large shrimp. When found on an Italian-American menu, it usually refers to a dish that includes shrimp cooked in garlic, butter, and lemon. At Paulie's, we do something similar, but of course we incorporate pasta.

» *This recipe will serve two.*

Ingredients

12 jumbo shrimp, cleaned, deveined, and butterflied

3 oz green onions, chopped

2 garlic cloves, sliced

Juice of 1 lemon

2 tbsp unsalted butter

3 tbsp olive oil

½ cup Bob's Red Mill all-purpose flour

¼ cup dry white wine

Kosher salt

Ground black pepper

½ lb fettuccini (see page 137)

Directions

1. Bring a pot of lightly salted water to a boil. I like to salt my water with 2 tablespoons for a large pot. Once water is boiling, add pasta. Cook until al dente. At the restaurant, we make our own pasta, which cooks in 4–5 minutes. Dry pasta will take 15–20 minutes.

2. Heat olive oil over medium-low heat in a sauté pan. Season shrimp with salt and pepper and dredge in flour. Shake off any excess flour.

3. Add shrimp to the pan of heated oil and sauté until firm, approximately 2 minutes. Add onion and garlic and sauté another 2 minutes. Carefully discard oil and deglaze pan with wine.

4. Add lemon juice and butter. Simmer until sauce thickens. Remove pan from heat and add pasta. Toss well and transfer to two serving bowls. Enjoy!

Paulie's Marinara

Our marinara has become our mother sauce. It's great simply mixed with pasta, or tossed with sausage and pickled vegetables. It's not spicy, but has a perfect acidity from the tomatoes. We use three types of tomatoes: ground, peeled strips, and roasted. The ground and peeled strips can be store bought in a can. Roasting tomatoes removes some of their liquid, intensifying their flavor. If you don't want to take the time, I like Mezzetta brand sauces, especially Calabrian Chili & Garlic. They are in most major grocery stores.

» *This is a batch recipe, so it should last at least a few meals.*

Ingredients

3 tbsp olive oil for sautéing

4 oz yellow onion, diced

1 tsp black pepper

2 garlic cloves, diced

24 oz peeled tomato strips (can)

12 oz ground tomatoes (can)

1 tsp dry oregano

1 tsp salt

1 lb roasted tomatoes, puréed (recipe below)

Directions

1. Heat 3 tablespoons oil over medium-low heat in large saucepan or stockpot. Add onions and black pepper. As onions soften, add garlic and cook until onions become clear.

2. Add the ground tomatoes and the peeled tomatoes. Stir well to combine. Add salt, oregano, and the roasted tomato purée.

3. Cover and cook over medium-low heat for about 45 minutes, stirring often to prevent sticking.

4. Remove from heat to cool and purée marinara thoroughly.

Roasted Tomatoes

Ingredients

2-3 lb Roma tomatoes

½ cup olive oil

2 tbsp dry basil

1 tbsp ground black pepper

Directions

1. Preheat oven to 425°F. Slice Roma tomatoes in half, and remove guts with a spoon (seeds and pulp).

2. Lay skin down on lined baking sheet. Drizzle olive oil and sprinkle with black pepper and dry basil.

3. "Bake" for about 25-30 minutes, or until dryness and shrinkage appear. You want to excrete some water, but don't leave the tomatoes completely dried out. Lay out to cool. These can be covered and refrigerated for several days. These are also great on sandwiches!

Creste di Gallo with Marinara and Sausage

....

Creste di gallo is one of my favorite pasta shapes; it means "rooster crest." As cool as it looks, it's also quite functional, as sauce is able to seep into its hollow ridges. A former employee, Sarah Troxell, developed this particular recipe. Thank you, chef!

» *This will serve two.*

Ingredients

1 cup Paulie's Marinara
(see page 10)

½ lb creste di gallo pasta, or
another hollow-shaped pasta
(see page 137)

2 links Italian sausage, cooked
and chopped

1 tsp red pepper flakes, adjusted
for desired spice level

4 large leaves fresh basil,
chiffonade

1 small purple onion

1 cup champagne vinegar

Kosher salt

¼ cup grated Parmesan

For the Pickled Onion

This is a quick and easy way to quickly pickle thinly sliced onions. Make this your first step in the recipe, and they may be ready by the time you finish cooking the other components of the dish. You can also start this earlier in the day if you want the flavor of the onions to be more acidic.

1. Using a mandoline, thinly slice the onion, then drench with champagne vinegar and sprinkle with salt. Mix well and cover. Because the slices are thin, it shouldn't take long for the onion to absorb the vinegar. You will have some left over for future use or for other dishes that need a little acidity.

Creste di Gallo with Marinara and Sausage

1. Bring a pot of lightly salted water to a boil. Drop pasta in and cook until al dente.

2. In a large sauté pan, heat marinara over low heat. Add sausage, red pepper flakes, basil, and pickled onions.

3. Add pasta to marinara and mix well. Transfer to two serving bowls and top with grated Parmesan.

Lobster Ravioli

The sugarosa makes this dish very rich and decadent. You may substitute Paulie's Marinara alone, instead of cream sauce, for a cleaner taste. It reminds me of the old-school Italian white-tablecloth restaurants. I use parsley in this recipe because of its nutritional value, and it doesn't have a strong fragrance that will get lost or cover up other ingredients. I also like it for the added color.

» *This will serve two.*

Ingredients

- 1 batch egg pasta dough (see page 137)
- ¼ lb unsalted butter (1 stick) at room temp
- 1 fresh lobster tail
- 4 oz whole-milk ricotta
- Juice of ½ lemon (no seeds)
- 3 garlic cloves, peeled and minced
- ⅛ cup freshly grated Parmesan
- ½ pint heavy cream
- ¼ cup Paulie's Marinara (see page 10)
- Freshly ground pepper
- Kosher salt
- 2 tbsp fresh parsley, chopped (set aside a few sprigs for garnish)

Ravioli Filling

1. Bring large pot of lightly salted water to a boil.

2. Cut through the top of the lobster shell lengthwise. Pull the shells slightly apart from the meat. This will let the meat expand when cooking.

3. Cook tails for about 3–4 minutes, making sure they are submerged. To check for doneness, cut into bottom of shell. If the meat is solid white with no opaqueness, they're done. If it seems a little opaque, let the tails cook another minute. It's important not to overcook, because they will continue to cook in the ravioli. Let tails cool, then remove meat and chop into small pieces.

4. Place ½ stick butter in a small saucepan over medium-low heat. Whisk the butter until browning appears, about 5 minutes. Remove from heat immediately and continue to whisk for another 30 seconds. Whisk in the garlic, and then stir in the chopped lobster.

5. Transfer to mixing bowl. Add chopped parsley, lemon juice, salt, and pepper. Add the ricotta cheese and mix well. Set the filling aside.

Ravioli

1. Roll out pasta dough per instructions all the way through #6 setting (see page 136). Lay out one sheet on well-floured surface.

2. Spoon quarter-sized dollops about 2 inches apart down the center of the sheet. Dip a pastry brush (or your finger) into water and make wet squares around each dollop. Lay a second sheet over your first sheet. Make sure to seal by pressing lightly along the wet areas. Also, make sure to squeeze out any air before completely sealing.

3. With a pasta cutter or pizza wheel, as evenly as possible, cut out your ravioli. Make sure to keep the surface and the ravioli lightly floured to prevent sticking. Before dropping the ravioli into boiling water, I like to brush off any of the excess flour. Remember, practice makes perfect!

4. Cook in lightly salted boiling water for about 2 minutes, or until they rise to the top and become firm. Remove with slotted spoon and plate when ready.

Sugarosa

My great-grandmother made sugarosa, which means "pink sauce," when I was a kid. To make it, we're going to add a bit of Paulie's Marinara to Alfredo sauce until we reach a rich pink color. Make Alfredo, add a bit of marinara, and you get sugarosa.

1. Add heavy cream and rest of butter to sauté pan. Heat over medium heat until butter melts. Add Parmesan and stir until sauce thickens. Stir in marinara a little bit at a time until you reach a light pink color.

2. Plate the ravioli individually on serving plates and ladle sugarosa sauce over ravioli. Finish with freshly ground black pepper and parsley sprigs.

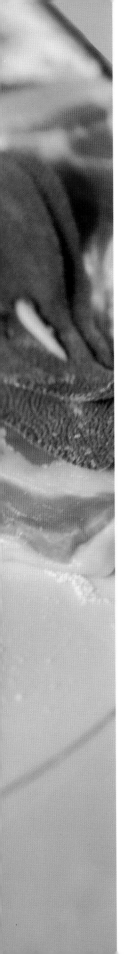

Veal Saltimbocca

Saltimbocca is a dish that originated in Rome, addressed as Saltimbocca alla Romana. It has been around for hundreds of years, with different variations and components. For this recipe, we will be using thin, tender veal. It can also be prepared with a thinly pounded chicken breast.

» *This recipe serves one.*

Ingredients

6 oz veal slice (or 8 oz chicken breast pounded thinly and evenly)

1 thin slice of prosciutto (translucent)

2 thin slices fresh mozzarella

3 tbsp olive oil

1 large garlic clove, sliced

3 oz chicken stock (see page 106)

3 oz dry Marsala wine

1 tbsp unsalted butter

Juice of half a lemon

2 fresh sage leaves

Kosher salt

Freshly ground pepper

½ cup Bob's Red Mill all-purpose flour

Directions

1. Heat olive oil in sauté pan over medium-low heat.

2. Salt and pepper both sides of veal (or chicken) and dredge in flour.

3. Lay the prosciutto on top of the veal, then lay sage leaves on top of the prosciutto. Secure with a toothpick.

4. Sauté in oil, veal side down, until ¾ done. Be careful with veal, as it is easy to overcook.

5. Drain off oil. Add Marsala to pan to deglaze. Add chicken stock, garlic, and lemon juice.

6. Place fresh mozzarella on top of prosciutto, trying not to touch the pan. Add butter to pan to thicken sauce.

7. Once sauce thickens, plate and remove toothpick, then pour sauce over. You can remove the veal and plate while sauce is still thickening to prevent overcooking.

Puttanesca

....

There are a couple of different stories behind the origin of Puttanesca. The most interesting story is that it originated from prostitutes trying to lure in clients with the pungent aromas of the ingredients. The ladies of the night would open a window to let the smells of the garlic and anchovy roam the streets and catch a sailor's nose. This dish definitely has strong flavors and is not for the faint of heart. I personally love it. A former employee, Sarah Troxell, developed the recipe we serve at Paulie's. Thank you, chef!

» *This will serve two.*

Ingredients

¼ lb bucatini or spaghetti
   (see page 137)

3 oz olive oil

3 cloves garlic, sliced

3 oz red onion, sliced

3 oz capers

¼ cup dry white wine

4 anchovy fillets, or
   2 oz anchovy paste

1 cup peeled tomato strips,
   available in can

3 oz pitted Kalamata olives, sliced

1 tbsp fresh oregano

4 leaves fresh basil, chiffonade

4 oz ricotta salata cheese

Directions

1. Bring pot of lightly salted water to boil. Drop pasta in and cook until al dente. Keep about ½ cup of pasta water.

2. In sauté pan, heat oil over medium-low heat. Add garlic, onion, and capers. Cook about 2 minutes. Deglaze with white wine.

3. Add tomatoes and anchovy, then reduce. Add olives, oregano, and basil.

4. Add pasta and about ¼ cup pasta water. Reduce further. The starch in the pasta water will help emulsify the sauce.

5. Separate into two serving bowls. Finish with crumbled ricotta salata.

Chicken Picatta
with Spaghetti Caesar

This has been on the Paulie's menu since day one, and it is easily one of our best sellers. I love acidity, so the lemon and wine in this dish really appeal to me. The spaghetti Caesar is actually something I came up with in the early years of Paulie's. We have such a good Caesar dressing that I wanted to use it on something other than lettuce. One day, I added it to pasta, threw in some olives and roasted tomatoes that were on the mise en place for the day. Voilà!

» *This is one serving at the restaurant, but could also feed two.*

Ingredients

1 8 oz chicken breast, pounded evenly

¼ cup dry white wine

1 tbsp unsalted butter

Juice of half a lemon

Kosher salt

Ground black pepper

½ cup Bob's Red Mill all-purpose flour

1 tbsp chopped parsley

4 tbsp olive oil

4 oz spaghetti (see page 137)

6 pitted Kalamata olives, halved

2 halves Paulie's roasted tomatoes, chopped (see page 10)

2 tbsp Paulie's Caesar Dressing (see page 24)

Directions

1. Pound the chicken breast so that it is even throughout, but not too thin. Season both sides with salt and pepper and dredge with flour.

2. Heat olive oil in sauté pan over medium heat. While oil is heating, bring lightly salted pot of water to boil for the pasta.

3. Drop spaghetti in boiling water. Remember, fresh pasta will only need a few minutes to cook; dry pasta will take much longer. If using dry pasta, bring water to boil before heating oil.

4. Shake any excess flour off the chicken and slowly lay the breast away from you into the pan. If there is no sizzle, remove chicken and wait for oil to reach a higher temperature. If the oil is not hot enough, the chicken will become saturated with oil. Sauté for 2–3 minutes and flip. I like a light golden color on the chicken; dark brown spots indicate burning, which creates a bitter flavor.

5. Once golden on each side, pour out cooking oil, return to heat, and add wine. Scrape any bits from the pan to incorporate into wine for added flavor. Lower heat to medium-low. Add lemon juice, butter, a touch of salt, and parsley. Let simmer until sauce thickens. Chicken will continue to cook; it's okay to remove chicken and let it rest on a plate while sauce is emulsifying to prevent overcooking. Pour sauce over chicken breast when ready.

6. Don't forget about your pasta. When ready, strain and transfer to mixing bowl. Add chopped roasted tomatoes, sliced olives, and Caesar dressing. Start with small amount of dressing, mix, and then add more if desired.

7. Add spaghetti Caesar to plate with Picatta. Enjoy!

Paulie's Caesar Dressing

This recipe batch is smaller than our usual batch size at the restaurant, but still large enough to last a few weeks. Use on your pasta or a salad. If oil starts to settle to the bottom, give it a good shake or mix, and it's good to go.

Ingredients

- 2 garlic cloves, peeled
- 1 tbsp ground black pepper
- 1 tsp kosher salt
- 1 tbsp Colman's mustard powder
- 1 oz anchovy paste
- 4 oz fresh lemon juice
- 12 oz grated Parmesan cheese
- 24 oz extra virgin olive oil

Directions

1. Place all ingredients *except* olive oil in food processor.

2. Process until well blended, stop, and push ingredients down if needed.

3. While processing slowly, add olive oil in a very slow stream. Remove from processor and store in airtight container.

> "The restaurant employees worked hard and played hard."

Charles Petronella, Nash D'Amico, Damian Mandola and Phillip Barletta at Damian's in Huntsville, TX c 1975

▲ Left to right: Charles Petronella, Nash D'Amico, Damian Mandola, and Phillip Barletta at Damian's, in Huntsville, Texas, circa 1975.

CHAPTER 2

Italian-American Italian

I'm often asked the difference between Italian-American and authentic Italian cooking. The answer is pretty simple. If you visit Italy, you will usually find the dishes to be very uncomplicated, unlike many Italian-American dishes, sometimes composed of only two or three ingredients. Italians value the ingredients as they are. They don't like to compromise Mother Nature's beauty. A protein (meat or fish) is seasoned well, typically enhanced by fresh herbs. The carb portion of the meal (pasta or risotto) is also usually pretty simple, sometimes with only fresh seafood or a vegetable and olive oil to enhance the dish. Italians are known for using what is available in their immediate geographical surroundings. It is the truest form of eating local. If it doesn't thrive in the region, it usually doesn't make it to the kitchen, which is one of the many reasons I love eating in Italy.

Grilled Whole Fish with Herbs

Branzino is a popular sea bass found in Italy; it is typically lean and flaky. You can substitute similar fish—domestic sea bass, trout, flounder, or red snapper would be my choice. We get tons of red snapper from the Gulf of Mexico. This recipe is a great example of local Italian cooking—fresh, simple, and delicious.

Ingredients

- 1 large red snapper, cleaned, gutted, and descaled; head and tail on
- 1 bunch fresh thyme
- 4 bay leaves
- 1 bunch fresh sage
- 2 garlic cloves, diced
- Extra virgin olive oil
- Kosher salt
- Ground black pepper
- 2 lemons, 1 sliced

Directions

1. Preheat grill to medium-high. Lightly brush with olive oil.

2. Lightly brush outside of fish with olive oil. Season fish with salt and pepper, inside and out. Stuff lemon slices into fish cavity along with thyme, bay leaves, and sage. Sprinkle diced garlic into cavity and rub on outside of fish.

3. Grill for about 5-7 minutes on each side, turning only once. Skin should release nicely from grill when ready. The hot grill will create a nice crispy skin.

4. Transfer to large plate, squeeze rest of lemon over fish, and enjoy family style!

Mushroom Risotto

Risotto is no doubt a staple in the motherland, but it can vary depending on your star ingredients. I'm using a dry white wine here, but it's not uncommon to use a dry red to pair with the earthy mushrooms. I like using shiitake and crimini mushrooms.

» *Serves two to three.*

Ingredients

4 cups chicken broth
  (see brodo, page 106)
2 tbsp olive oil
½ onion, chopped
1 cup Arborio rice
½ cup dry white wine
½ cup grated Parmesan
1 tbsp unsalted butter
2 tbsp chopped parsley
1 lb mushrooms, sliced
Kosher salt
Ground black pepper

Directions

1. In small saucepan, bring chicken broth to simmer, not a boil. It's important to keep the broth hot as you add to the risotto later.

2. Sauté chopped onion in olive oil in thick pot over medium heat. Season with salt and pepper. When onions become translucent, add rice and cook for about 1 minute, constantly stirring.

3. Add wine; cook until wine is absorbed, about 2 minutes. Continue to stir, preventing rice from sticking. Add 1 cup of hot chicken broth and stir. Reduce heat to low and cover with lid. Check back frequently; as broth is absorbed, continue to add 1 cup of broth at a time until rice is done, taste for density.

4. In sauté pan, sauté mushrooms in butter. Season with salt and pepper. When mushrooms are fully cooked, fold into risotto. Ideally, you want to time the mushrooms and risotto to be ready at the same time.

5. Add Parmesan and parsley to risotto, mix well, and serve.

When my great-grandparents first came to America in the early 1900s, they couldn't believe how available every kind of food was in the United States. America was more integrated, with less focus on the specific regions, and you could find many fruits, vegetables, and herbs year-round. Because ingredients were more readily available, immigrants learned to make richer sauces and to use more ingredients. This abundance taught them to cook larger portions and to smother them in sauces and elements that would be too expensive in the Old Country. Alfredo sauce, for example, is thought to have originated in Rome in the early 1900s, but it took off in America, where cream, butter, and cheese were more readily available. I also credit my great-grandparents with introducing me to the evolution of authentic Italian cooking into Italian-American cooking. Our Sunday suppers usually consisted of pasta with homemade sauce and stuffed artichokes, but we also had fried chicken or chicken soup. It was a time when going to the farmers' market was an event everyone looked forward to.

Authentic Italian food varies throughout Italy. Each region has its own cheeses, meats, vegetables, seafood, and wine grape varieties. Typically, Northern Italy uses butter more often than olive oil for cooking. There's more wild game in the countryside, so it ends up more often on the plate, along with amazing mushrooms and truffles.

The Friuli region produces what some consider Italy's best prosciutto, Prosciutto di San Daniele. Prosciutto is made only from pigs raised in Italy and sea salt—no other preservatives or additives are added. The pigs are never frozen. They must reach San Daniele quickly for processing, so they usually come from nearby.

Liguria is known for basil pesto—one of my favorites!

Rice and polenta are seen more in the Northern regions, along with hearty soups, due to the colder climates. Pasta is available throughout Italy, but fresh pasta made from flour and eggs is seen more in the north.

As you move south, you will see well-known items like Parmigiano-Reggiano, Bolognese sauce, balsamic vinegar, and Prosciutto di Parma. Prosciutto di Parma is made using the same standards as prosciutto from San Daniele. The biggest difference is the origin of the pigs. All the pigs must be from Italy, but the different regions mean different diets and climate conditions. Both prosciuttos are made with only sea salt, air, and time to cure the hams. The pigs in Parma are often fed cheese rinds from Parmigiano-Reggiano.

Farther south and into Sicily, you see more lemon orchards, buffalo mozzarella, and the popular Neapolitan-style pizza. The pasta in the South is mostly dry, made from hard flour and water. The majority is still handmade, then dried for preservation.

My family is actually from Sicily. If you ask most mainland Italians, they will tell you that Sicily is a separate country. It's a unique region. Sicily is the home of Mount Etna, an active volcano that produces nutritious volcanic soil—great for citrus orchards, olives, and grapes.

Most Sicilians seem to have entered the United States through the Gulf of Mexico, as opposed to Ellis Island, in New York, like most Italian immigrants. My family left Corleone, Sicily, and made their claim in Houston and Galveston.

Fettuccini Alfredo

Alfredo sauce is the macaroni and cheese of Italian-American cooking. It is also a staple on the Paulie's menu, and I'm not sure I could ever remove it. Much like other Italian dishes, it's made from simple ingredients, but it takes practice to perfect the creamy texture.

» *This will serve two.*

Ingredients

½ lb fettuccini (see page 137)

½ cup heavy whipping cream

2 tbsp unsalted butter

¼ cup grated Parmesan

Directions

1. Bring pot of lightly salted water to boil. Drop in pasta. Cook until al dente.

2. In sauté pan over medium-low heat, add butter and cream. Stir until butter is melted.

3. Add Parmesan and stir continuously. As cheese melts, the texture will thicken. You don't want the cheese to burn. Once you have the desired creaminess, remove pan from heat. If it's too thick, you can add more cream. If it's too thin, add more cheese.

4. Add fettuccini to pan and toss. Separate into two serving bowls and top with more Parmesan, if desired.

Chicken Parmesan

At Paulie's, we panfry the chicken rather than deep-frying it. That means we use fresh oil every time. It makes a difference in flavor. Fryer oil can take on flavors of other items that have been dropped in that day. It can also start to burn if not changed frequently. We don't want those flavors transferred to our chicken.

» *This is one serving at Paulie's but can easily feed two.*

Ingredients

1 8 oz chicken breast, pounded evenly

2 eggs

½ cup Bob's Red Mill all-purpose flour

½ cup seasoned Italian breadcrumbs

1 cup canola fry oil

2 slices low-moisture mozzarella (deli style)

¼ cup Paulie's Marinara (see page 10)

2 tbsp grated Parmesan

Kosher salt

Ground black pepper

Directions

1. Preheat oven to 325°F. In large skillet or sauté pan, heat oil over medium-high heat. Based on your skillet size, you may need more oil. You want the chicken submerged.

2. Season chicken breast with salt and pepper on both sides. Beat eggs in large bowl.

3. Dredge seasoned chicken in flour, shake off excess flour and dredge in egg, then coat chicken in breadcrumbs in a separate bowl. To make it easy, have your bowls of flour, egg, and breadcrumbs next to each other and go through like an assembly line.

4. On the line, we check the oil temperature by barely touching the chicken to the oil. If there's no sizzle, it's not hot enough yet. No need to raise the flame; try giving it a few more minutes. If it sizzles violently and sprays, it may be too hot. Lower heat a little and wait a minute.

5. Fry breast on both sides for about 2–3 minutes each. I like a light golden brown without any indication of uncooked chicken. Dark brown or black around the edges indicates burning. Those edges will have a bitter flavor.

6. Discard frying oil and keep breast in the pan. Spoon marinara over breast, top with mozzarella, then sprinkle Parmesan over the top.

7. Pop in the oven to simply melt the cheeses and finish cooking chicken, 1–2 minutes. Remove when cheese melts and transfer to serving plate.

8. At Paulie's, we serve with a side of spaghetti marinara. Simply toss cooked spaghetti with Paulie's Marinara and add to serving plate.

Pesto

....

Our pesto at Paulie's may be my favorite dish of all time. I remember first tasting it as a kid. I couldn't get enough of it. Pesto sauce is something you can make ahead of time and keep refrigerated for future use. Boil some pasta, add pesto, mix, and you're done.

» *This batch recipe should last a few meals.*

Ingredients

⅓ cup pine nuts, lightly toasted

1 tsp kosher salt

½ tsp ground black pepper

3 cloves garlic

3 cups fresh basil, firmly packed

¼ cup extra virgin olive oil

¼ cup grated Parmesan

Directions

1. Place pine nuts, salt, and pepper in food processor and process until finely ground.

2. Add garlic, basil, and small amount of olive oil. Process until finely ground.

3. While still processing, pour in rest of oil very slowly.

4. Add Parmesan slowly and process until mixed well and pesto sauce is smooth.

Fusilli Pesto

....

» *This will serve two.*

Ingredients

¼ cup pesto

½ lb fusilli pasta (see page 137)

1 tbsp toasted pine nuts

1 tbsp Kalamata olives, halved

1 tbsp grated Parmesan

Directions

1. Bring pot of lightly salted water to a boil, add pasta, and cook until al dente. Drain and transfer to mixing bowl.

2. Spoon in about ¼ cup of pesto and mix well. More can be added to preference.

3. Transfer to two serving bowls. Top with pine nuts, olives, and Parmesan.

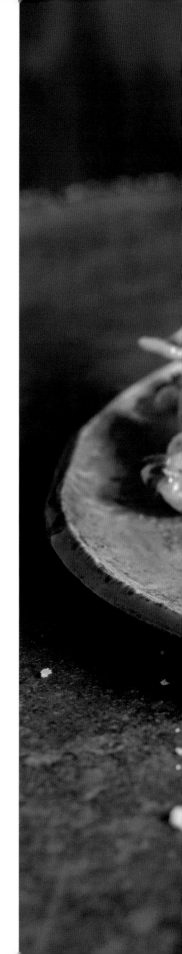

Rigatoni Bolognese

Bolognese is a hearty Italian dish that can fill your stomach and warm your heart. This is one of the recipes given to us by Terrence Gallivan and Seth Siegel-Gardner from The Pass & Provisions. At the restaurant, we use batch recipes that feed several people at a time.

» *This recipe serves three to four.*

Ingredients

- 2 cloves garlic, peeled
- ¼ yellow onion, peeled and roughly chopped
- 1 small carrot, peeled and roughly chopped
- 1 celery stalk, cleaned and roughly chopped
- 3 tbsp olive oil
- ½ lb ground veal
- ¼ lb ground beef
- ¼ cup dry red wine
- 2 tbsp red wine vinegar
- 1 tbsp tomato paste
- ¼ cup heavy cream
- ½ cup grated Parmesan
- 5-6 fresh basil leaves, chiffonade
- Kosher salt
- ½ lb rigatoni pasta (see page 137)

Directions

1. At the restaurant, we roughly mince the vegetables in a food processor to make soffritto (which is similar to mirepoix in French cooking), but you can easily use a chef knife. Heat the olive oil in a large saucepan or sauté pan over medium heat. Add vegetables to pan once oil reaches temperature. Let the vegetables slowly caramelize, approximately 5 minutes. Stir occasionally.

2. Bring pot of lightly salted water to boil. Drop in pasta and cook until al dente.

3. When the vegetables are caramelized, add the veal and beef and let the meat brown. It's important not to cook the meat all the way through at this point. It will continue to cook as we finish the ragù.

4. Once meat is browned on the outside, deglaze the pan with red wine and vinegar. Stir well to loosen any bits on the bottom of the pan. Add tomato paste and lower heat. Simmer for 10-15 minutes while stirring. Add cream and simmer for another 10-15 minutes, or until the desired consistency is achieved. More cream can be added if desired. Add salt to taste.

5. Before straining your pasta, add a few tablespoons of pasta water to your ragù while it's simmering. This will help marry all of your ingredients together and create a really nice consistency. Add pasta to the ragù. Toss well and plate. Garnish with fresh basil and Parmesan.

Cuccidati Cookies

All of you Catholic Italians out there know these as the St. Joseph's altar cookies, or Sicilian fig cookies. These are also a Christmas tradition in my family. I first started making these with my great-grandmother Maw-maw Lamonte when I was in elementary school. These cookies are a great way for kids to learn basic baking skills.

» *This recipe will make about 2 dozen. If baking for the holidays, you'll want to double (or triple) the amounts!*

For the Dough

2 cups Bob's Red Mill baking flour

2 tsp baking powder

Pinch salt

¼ cup granulated sugar

½ cup vegetable shortening (Crisco)

1 egg

¼ cup milk

1 tsp vanilla extract

For the Filling

½ cup dry figs

½ cup dried dates, pitted

¼ cup raisins

¼ cup pecan pieces

2 tbsp apricot preserves (I prefer Bonne Maman brand)

For the Icing

1 cup confectioners' sugar

½ tsp vanilla extract

2 tbsp milk

Colored sprinkles (for kids)

Directions

1. Sift the flour, baking powder, and salt in large mixing bowl. Add sugar and mix well.

2. Work in the shortening with fork.

3. In separate bowl, beat the egg, milk, and vanilla.

4. Combine wet and dry ingredients and beat for several minutes, until dough is formed.

5. Knead the dough with your hands for another 5 minutes.

6. Split the dough into two pieces, wrap with plastic, and let stand for 30–45 minutes. If you doubled the recipe, separate into four pieces.

7. Finely chop the figs, dates, raisins, and pecans. Add to mixing bowl and add preserves. Mix well, until ingredients are incorporated. The preserves will act as the glue. Set aside.

8. Preheat oven to 375°F. Line a cookie sheet with parchment paper.

9. With a rolling pin, roll out dough to no thicker than ¼ inch. Do your best to roll out the dough into a square shape. You can roll dough between two pieces of parchment paper, if you want to cut down on flour mess. Cut the square in half horizontally, left to right. Along the center of each piece, fill with fig mixture. Roll into a nice tight log, sealing along the center and on the ends. Place the seam facing down.

10. Cut cookies from the log, about 2 inches in width each. You can cut off the ends if they are too doughy. Also, cut three slits on one side of each cookie. Place cookies on baking sheet and fan out the side with slits. Bake for about 15–20 minutes, or until golden brown.

11. Let cookies cool. Then make icing combining confectioners' sugar, milk, and vanilla. Mix well, making sure it's not too runny. Brush the top of each cookie with icing. If adding sprinkles, do so right away. I prefer no sprinkles, but loved them as a kid. Enjoy!

Stuffed Artichokes

If any recipe reminds me of my great-grandmother, it is stuffed artichokes. She was a perfectionist at these. Stuffed artichokes bring back many memories from Sunday supper. I don't know many other five-year-olds who would finish a whole artichoke alone. The reward was always the artichoke heart after all the leaves were plucked and eaten.

» *Serves four.*

Ingredients

4 medium artichokes

½ lemon

1 cup Italian seasoned breadcrumbs

½ cup grated Parmesan

¼ cup chopped parsley

2 cloves garlic, minced

Kosher salt

Fresh ground pepper

Extra virgin olive oil

Directions

1. Preheat oven to 400°F. Cut stems from artichokes; leave the bottom level so they stand up on their own. Remove tough outer leaves. Using serrated knife, cut about 1 inch off the tops of each choke.

2. Wash artichokes well; let dry upside down. Rub tops of leaves with lemon to prevent browning. Spread leaves as open as possible without breaking.

3. Combine breadcrumbs, Parmesan, parsley, and garlic. Season with salt and pepper and toss well.

4. With a spoon, stuff each artichoke with filling, trying to get between all leaves. Close leaves gently. Add about 1 inch of water to deep baking pan or pot. For added flavor in the hearts, substitute chicken broth (see page 106) for water. Arrange the artichokes closely and drizzle tops with olive oil.

5. Cover completely with aluminum foil and bake at 400°F for 3 hours. It is important the hearts steam well and soften; in the meantime the breadcrumbs and cheese will bake and become delicious.

6. Baste the tops occasionally; add more water to pan if need be. Test for doneness by pulling off lower outer leaves to check for softness.

7. Remember, the goal is getting to the artichoke heart. After you peel and eat all the outer leaves, you will run into fuzz. Remove the fuzz and uncover what is the sweet spot of the choke! Enjoy!

Pasta con Sarde

This is a very Sicilian dish, often called the official dish of Sicily. Former staff member Felipe Riccio put this particular preparation on the Paulie's menu. Felipe is a chef but moved to working in the wine bar as a sommelier to expand his repertoire. Felipe and his wife Hayley moved to Italy in 2016. Thanks, chef!

» *Serves two.*

Ingredients

1 whole sardine, 2-3 oz, filleted

2 tbsp ricotta salata, crumbled

½ lb bucatini pasta or spaghetti
(see page 137)

¼ cup panko breadcrumbs

1 tbsp parsley, chopped

Juice of ½ lemon

Zest of 1 lemon

2 tbsp olive oil

1 tsp freshly cracked black pepper

1 garlic clove, minced

2 tbsp unsalted butter

Pinch kosher salt

8-10 halves pickled cherry tomatoes
(see page 74)

Directions

1. Bring pot of lightly salted water to boil, drop in pasta, and cook until al dente. Save a bit of pasta water for later use.

2. In small mixing bowl, combine sardine fillets with lemon zest, parsley, garlic, salt, and black pepper.

3. In sauté pan, toast the breadcrumbs in 1 tablespoon butter over low heat until brown. Transfer breadcrumbs to separate bowl.

4. Wipe out any breadcrumbs left behind and return sauté pan to medium heat. Heat olive oil until hot. Add sardine mixture and cook for about 2-3 minutes. Add pasta along with a touch of pasta water. Add fresh lemon juice and the other 1 tablespoon of butter.

5. After sauce thickens, separate pasta into two bowls. Top with ricotta salata, pickled tomatoes, and breadcrumbs. Enjoy!

CHAPTER 3

Opening Paulie's

My father, Bernard, and my stepmother, Kathy, developed a business plan for their own restaurant in the 1990s. I remember the day a name was chosen for the restaurant: Paulie's, after me. I was flattered that they thought that much of me, but I was also wary of what this could mean for my future. Was this the seed being planted for me to someday take over the family business?

Other than roaming the premises and soaking up the aromas as a kid, I had shown no interest in the restaurant business at this point. I wasn't involved in the planning; I was in college in San Marcos, Texas, and honestly, I never thought I would choose this career path. I was in business school, majoring in marketing. Having grown up around restaurants, I knew the struggles of the industry and how taxing it can be on families. I wanted to make sure the career I chose was going to make me happy and healthy. I wanted a corporate job with benefits, vacation, and weekends off.

Before Paulie's, my parents had both worked really hard and for a long time in the food industry. My father catered for Ninfa's, a wildly successful Mexican food chain in Houston, for over ten years after my uncle's restaurants closed, and Kathy was heavily involved in the grocery store and deli concept Butera's. They were both used to blue-collar jobs with modest pay.

Because of this humble background, I wasn't sure I was going to have the opportunity to attend college. When I applied for school, I didn't expect to attend the University of Texas or A&M—or even to get accepted. It was one of those "let's just see" moments. I knew Stephen F. Austin or Southwest Texas State were more realistic. I was surprisingly accepted into Texas A&M, the University of Texas, Stephen F. Austin, and Southwest Texas State. A good number of my friends were attending Southwest Texas, so that's where I went. Between financial aid, a (very) small scholarship, working summers, working at school, and as much help from my parents as possible, I was off to college!

Pimento Cheese

Kathy Petronella worked at Butera's deli for several years in the 1980s, helping develop and implement recipes. One of these was the pimento cheese sandwich. First, we'll put together the pimento cheese, and then we'll build the sandwich like we do at Paulie's.

» *This batch should be enough for three to four sandwiches.*

Ingredients

¾ lb cheddar cheese

½ lb low-moisture mozzarella cheese (deli style)

2 oz green onions, chopped

3 oz roasted red bell peppers, finely chopped

1 tbsp roasted garlic

12 oz mayo

½ tsp black pepper

Kosher salt

Directions

1. Grate both cheeses onto a plate. Toss the cheeses with onions and red bell peppers. At the restaurant, we roast our own bell peppers, but you may buy roasted peppers in a can.

2. Add mayo and roasted garlic and combine thoroughly. We also roast our own garlic, but you can find it at the store as well.

3. Add salt and pepper to taste.

Pimento Cheese Sandwich

Ingredients

¼ cup pimento cheese

Challah buns, or white round buns, lightly toasted

1 tomato, sliced

1 leaf green leaf lettuce

Salt and pepper for seasoning

Directions

1. Spread pimento cheese generously on bottom bun. Because the pimento cheese contains mayo, I like to leave the bread dry.

2. Top with tomatoes (season with salt and pepper), lettuce, and top bun. Slice in half and enjoy!

Chicken Salad

The chicken salad recipe that we use at Paulie's is also one of Kathy's original recipes from Butera's. It's great on a sandwich or alone with a fork!

This recipe will make enough for two to three sandwiches.

Ingredients

- 3 chicken breasts, grilled and pulled into small pieces
- 2 oz celery, cleaned and chopped
- 2 oz dill pickles, chopped
- 1 oz green onions, finely chopped
- ¾ oz pecan pieces
- 1 tsp black pepper
- Kosher salt
- 7 oz mayo

Directions

1. In large mixing bowl, combine chicken pieces, celery, pickles, onions, pecans, and black pepper. Mix.

2. Add mayo and mix thoroughly.

3. Add salt and pepper to taste.

Chicken Salad Sandwich

Ingredients

- ¼ cup chicken salad
- Challah buns, or white round buns, lightly toasted
- 1 tomato, sliced
- 1 leaf green leaf lettuce
- Salt and pepper for seasoning

Directions

1. Generously spread chicken salad on bottom bun. The chicken salad contains mayo, so I like to leave the bread dry.

2. Top with sliced tomatoes and season with salt and pepper.

3. Add lettuce and then top bun. Slice and enjoy!

Grilled Portobello Sandwich

Kathy served a portobello sandwich at Butera's in the 1980s, but when she opened Paulie's, she spruced it up a bit. We're going to add grilled red bell pepper, goat cheese, and a Dijon-mayo spread. This is a great vegetarian sandwich.

» *This makes one sandwich.*

Ingredients

Challah bun, or wheat round bun

1 large portobello mushroom

½ red bell pepper

1 oz goat cheese

1 oz Dijon mustard

2 oz mayo

1 Roma tomato, sliced

1 leaf green leaf lettuce, washed

Kosher salt

Ground black pepper

2 tbsp olive oil

Directions

1. Preheat grill to medium heat. Remove stem from portobello and peel off dark layer from top of cap. Halve the bell pepper. Remove stem and guts. Dress both the portobello and ½ bell pepper with olive oil, salt, and pepper.

2. Toss on grill and cook on both sides until both are soft and pliable, about 5 minutes. The bell pepper may get black burn spots from the grill. You can simply peel that off once it cools.

3. Lightly toast your bun. Mix the Dijon and mayo together and spread on top side of bun. Spread goat cheese on the bottom half.

4. Start with bell pepper over the goat cheese, then mushroom, tomato, and lettuce. Top with bun, slice, and enjoy!

▼ Sketching out pie chart of general restaurant expenses.

I was two years into college when Paulie's opened, in April 1998. The spring semester had just ended, and my dad asked me to work the counter. As much as I wanted to say no, I couldn't. *What's the big deal?* I thought. *I'm just working at my family's restaurant during the summer; it's not my career.*

I was one of two cashiers on staff. The other was a very sweet woman named Rose. Otherwise, either my dad or stepmom would man the registers and then run back into the kitchen to make the order they just took.

You could hear crickets in there for the first few months, which caused tension and stress among the family. Every detail was scrutinized: what we said to customers, how we said it, overly generous portions, and the consistency of every plate. They had to give their employees pretty lean schedules during that time.

My parents emptied their bank accounts and took on a good deal of debt to open the restaurant. It was a big risk to take on in their forties. In their minds, this had to work. They couldn't go back to working for someone else after this.

This is a typical situation in an undercapitalized small business; I see it all the time in the restaurant industry. In most cases, inexperienced restaurateurs don't account for all the costs that restaurants incur to operate in the long term.

Initially, they promise employees high wages, insurance, great hours, a creative work environment—yay!

Trust me, we all want to give our employees six figures, full health coverage, paid vacations, and retirement funds, but the reality is that most restaurants, especially independent restaurants, simply can't afford this.

There is a financial formula to most restaurants: Typically, an average restaurant should shoot for spending 30–40 percent on food and beverage costs. A full-service restaurant will need a substantial number of employees, which can account for another 30–40 percent of costs.

Negotiating a fair long-term deal on your rental agreement can also be a deciding factor in how long your restaurant will succeed. Rental rates will almost always increase over time; they rarely go down. It is important to know that the rental rate fifteen to twenty years from your opening will still work within the business plan. A rate that is 5 percent or less of your total costs is ideal. Depending on your price per person, a rate closer to 10 percent may also work. A higher rate is more likely to work in a high-profile dining concept.

Most restaurants have costs like utilities, paper goods, cleaning supplies, smallwares, and insurance, but I don't think most people realize these necessities can account for 10–15 percent of your total costs. If you still make 5 percent profit, well, you are indeed a profitable business.

At Paulie's, we operate with food and beverage at about 40 percent of our costs. We offer value at an affordable price, so our food costs will never be exceptional. Our payroll costs are higher than average, at 40 percent, because we have a large staff, and I try to take care of them as well as possible. We no longer have bank loan payments, so that frees up 5 percent of the costs for a larger payroll. The rest of the monthly operating costs make up about 12–15 percent, which leaves 5–8 percent profit for Paulie's.

There are some months we may not make a profit at all. We may catch three payrolls in one month, or we'll need to purchase a large piece of equipment, or bad weather will interrupt sales. There are many unpredictable costs. This is why it is so important to stay open and available to your customer base.

It's also imperative to never get too comfortable making purchases. I aspire to practice a modest and healthy business model every month. I have heard people call me a slave driver or claim that I am running a sweatshop. Restaurants often need employees to work long hours; we work while others are eating and enjoying themselves. This is the industry we chose. Frankly, some of my staff need overtime hours to take care of their families. I need them to work, and they want to work. We are a family, and this is how we take care of each other.

New restaurants will usually attract great business because of the initial excitement, but that fades and the real work begins: figuring out how to stay consistent and relevant. After they spread themselves thin trying to keep all their previous promises, they may have a few bad months, realize the red line is getting closer, and start cutting costs. The first costs to go? Benefits. There's no more 401(k) and no more insurance. Their staff starts working longer hours for the same pay, and employee turnover increases.

I prefer to work in the opposite direction. I prefer to put you to work in the beginning, show you how this business actually works, and reward you from there within our financial capabilities. If you expect a Fortune 500 environment, this industry may not be for you. I try to prepare my people for the real world. Life is unpredictable, as is this industry. If you can move up in my businesses, you can succeed at anything in life.

My father instilled this culture of caution and responsible spending in us from the beginning. We couldn't guarantee customers would continue to walk through the doors every day, so we had to spend money only on things that would contribute directly to the business, nothing unnecessary. "If it still works, we're still using it," was the basic philosophy.

The biggest myth is that owners of small businesses are sitting on piles of money. This couldn't be further from the truth. Small business owners should know how much money is going out and how much is coming in at all times. This is how we determine when and how money can be spent. It's embarrassing when checks start to bounce because thousands were spent on new kitchen toys that are not necessary to implement the menu.

Are improvements necessary? Absolutely. Is remodeling after a certain period of time necessary? Absolutely. But your decisions have to be disciplined. Start a budget. After all the bills are paid and you still have a healthy bank account, put some of that into savings. Use that for improvements, new toys, and upgrades.

You have to take care of your employees and vendors before you start treating yourself. There were several times in Paulie's history when my parents or I could not pay ourselves because the bank account was getting thin. Because I continued my father's careful approach, I have never missed an employee payroll, nor are we in debt to any vendors.

Paulie's was eventually welcomed to the neighborhood, as you might imagine. About six months after opening, we received our first review from the *Houston Chronicle*, from food writer Kathi Mosbacher. Of course, there are always positive and negative elements of every review, but overall, it was positive and inspirational. Kathi was kind and over the years became a friend of ours.

After that day, Paulie's has seen consistent business. Severe weather and emergencies aside, we never had a day like those first six months again.

The day after the review, the ship was on high alert. We knew that our business depended on good reviews like this, but it was also high stress because of the inevitable increase in business. We knew we had to order more food. We knew we had to have all hands on deck. We knew we were about to get our asses kicked.

And we did.

The next day was a zoo. People were lining up at the door before we opened. Since we had not experienced this sort of volume before, we were unsure how Paulie's kitchen could handle it. It turns out that our setup sucks for high volume. Our menu is large, and our hot line is too small. It has to be one of the hardest line cook jobs around. Our cooks absolutely have to stay ahead of the ticket flow, or it can quickly turn into the *Titanic*. Once we get behind, trying to catch up is like swimming through quicksand.

▲ Paulie's first press! Left to right: Kathy Petronella, Paul Petronella, Bernard Petronella, circa 1998.

> **❝My father instilled this culture of caution and responsible spending in us from the beginning.❞**

Shrimp BLT

The Shrimp BLT has been on the menu for what seems like forever. And it will probably continue to be a staple on the menu. This is the sandwich that usually gets the attention of the press. The secret is the sauce we finish the shrimp in. I'm going to simplify it a bit for home preparation.

» *This will make two sandwiches.*

Ingredients

- 2 challah buns, or white buns
- 10 jumbo shrimp, cleaned, deveined, and butterflied
- 6 tbsp mayo
- 2 tbsp Dijon or spicy mustard
- 1 large tomato, sliced
- 2 large leaves green leaf lettuce, washed
- 4 slices cooked bacon, preferably smoky
- 3 tbsp olive oil
- 1 garlic clove, diced
- 2 tbsp unsalted butter
- Kosher salt
- Freshly ground pepper

Directions

1. In sauté pan, heat olive oil over medium-low heat. Season shrimp with salt and pepper. Sauté in oil for 2–3 minutes with the garlic, until they are pinkish and firm. Add butter and continue sautéing for another minute. Remove pan from heat when shrimp are fully cooked.

2. Toast the buns lightly. Mix the mayo and spicy mustard together and spread on both sides of the bread evenly.

3. Place bacon on the bottom half of each bun, then place 5 shrimp on top of the bacon. Next, add tomato slices. I like to salt and pepper the tomatoes. Finally, place lettuce leaf on top of tomatoes. Finish with top bun and slice sandwich through the middle. (We like to use long toothpicks to hold halves together at the restaurant.) Enjoy!

The Big Salad

"You had to have the BIG SALAD!" Our Big Salad is a take on a *Seinfeld* episode where Elaine orders a big salad with big vegetables. Our Big Salad is . . . pretty big, much like most of our food portions. The key to our salad is emulsified vinaigrette. At Paulie's, we intentionally want this dressing to be thick so that it adheres to the lettuce and all the vegetables, as opposed to sinking to the bottom of the bowl. Make a batch and save in the fridge for all of your salads.

» *This recipe should be enough for three to four salads.*

Ingredients

2 oz vinaigrette

½ head of romaine lettuce, washed and chopped

1 celery stalk, washed and chopped

1 carrot, peeled and chopped

1 large Roma tomato, quartered

½ avocado, peeled and sliced

2 oz feta cheese

½ cucumber, peeled and chopped

3 button mushrooms, cleaned and sliced

Directions

1. In large mixing bowl, combine lettuce, carrot, celery, cucumber, and mushrooms. Add a small amount of vinaigrette at a time and mix well.

2. Transfer to a serving bowl. Finish with tomatoes, sliced avocado, and feta. *Mangia!*

Paulie's Vinaigrette

Ingredients

⅓ cup Dijon mustard

3 oz red wine vinegar

5 cloves garlic

1 tbsp salt

1 tbsp black pepper

1½ cups extra virgin olive oil

2 cups vegetable oil

Directions

1. Place all ingredients in food processor, except olive oil and vegetable oil, and process until well blended.

2. The key to a well-emulsified texture is SLOWLY adding the oil while still blending. At the restaurant, we have a special funnel that has a pinhole. We pour the oils in the funnel while the processor is blending until all the oil is blended and the texture of the vinaigrette is thick. At home, you can very slowly pour in your oils.

Summer Salad

When I make a salad at home, it usually consists of arugula, cherry tomatoes, olive oil, lemon juice, salt, and pepper. At first, I thought this would be too simple for a restaurant menu. But after introducing it as a lunch special, I learned that people liked it enough for it to gain a spot on the menu. At the restaurant, I add grated pecorino, pickled tomatoes, cucumber, and a slice of fresh melon.

» *This recipe makes two salads.*

Ingredients

- 4 oz arugula, washed and dried
- 10 halves pickled cherry tomatoes
- ½ cucumber, peeled and sliced into half-moons
- Juice of ½ lemon
- 2 tbsp extra virgin olive oil
- 2 tbsp grated pecorino cheese
- 1 slice of fresh melon (watermelon, cantaloupe, or honeydew)
- 1 tsp kosher salt
- 1 tsp freshly cracked black pepper

Directions

1. In large mixing bowl, toss arugula and cucumbers with lemon juice, olive oil, salt, and pepper.

2. Separate onto two serving plates. Finish with pecorino and pickled tomatoes on top and slice of melon on the side. *Buon appetito!*

Pickled Cherry Tomatoes

Ingredients

- 4 cups vinegar
- 4 cups boiling water
- ½ cup sugar
- ½ cup kosher salt
- 5 cloves garlic, sliced
- 3 tbsp dried thyme
- 20-30 cherry tomatoes, sliced in half

Directions

1. In mixing bowl, combine sugar, salt, garlic, and thyme with boiling water. Stir until salt and sugar are completely dissolved. Let cool, then add vinegar. Finally, add tomatoes and pickle overnight. Tomatoes will last several weeks refrigerated.

Brined Pork Chop

Brining your meat before cooking it is a great way to ensure juicy and flavorful dishes, and pork chops can easily dry out during cooking. At the restaurant, we brine several pork racks at a time. At home, you can make enough brine for whatever you plan to cook, whether it's two chicken breasts, one pork chop, or a whole turkey.

Makes about ½ gallon of brine.

Ingredients for Brining Solution

¾ cup sugar

¾ cup kosher salt

3 cups boiling water

5 cups cold water

10 garlic cloves, sliced

1 tbsp cracked black pepper

1 tbsp fresh thyme

Directions

1. In a large mixing bowl, combine boiling water, sugar, salt, garlic, pepper, and thyme. Mix until all salt and sugar are dissolved. Let stand another 10 minutes to let flavors sit in hot water and infuse the brine. Finally, add 5 cups cold water.

2. In large-enough pot, or bowl, pour brine over meat. Make sure meat is completely submerged. You can double the recipe if you are brining something as large as a turkey, or cut recipe in half for something much smaller. It's important to keep the ratio of ingredients the same.

3. If brining a whole chicken, whole turkey, or whole pork rack, I suggest brining for about 24 hours. If brining something smaller like chicken legs or thighs, or single pork chops, simply letting it sit overnight is substantial. Remove pork chops from brine and pat dry. Preheat grill to medium-high heat. Grill approximately 3–4 minutes on each side of the chop, depending on thickness of cut. If you have a meat thermometer, I like to cook to 140°F internally and remove from heat. It will continue to cook a bit after you remove from heat.

   At the restaurant, our pork chop is served with a small arugula salad and new potatoes.

Fettuccini with Mussels

This dish was introduced at our Holcombe location, and then transferred to the Westheimer location when I made the move. It is currently our Friday night special and has been for several years. It's simple and briny, like the ocean. There is not much of a "sauce" in this one. After sautéing, we deglaze with dry sherry. As the alcohol burns off, the sherry, mussel ocean water, and olive oil become the coating for the fettuccini noodles.

» *This will serve two.*

Ingredients

2 lb mussels, scrubbed and debearded

½ lb fettuccini (see page 137)

2 large rosemary sprigs

¼ cup dry sherry

3 garlic cloves, sliced

2 oz green onion, chopped

2 tbsp olive oil

Directions

1. Soak the mussels in fresh water for about an hour before beginning. When alive, mussels will open and close slightly in water, allowing the fresh water to wash out any sand or grit inside.

2. Bring pot of lightly salted water to boil. Drop in pasta. Cook until al dente.

3. Cleaning mussels can be more difficult than expected, but it's important to clean thoroughly. The first step is removing the "beards," or the strings coming out of the shells. Pull these out with your hands, pulling toward the hinge. Next, scrub the barnacles off the shells. Sometimes this takes a little elbow grease. Mussel shells should be all black and shiny when clean. You don't want any barnacle pieces coming off in the sauté pan.

4. You will also need to remove any opened or cracked mussels; this usually signifies they are dead. You only want to cook live mussels. You can sometimes close an open mussel and it will stay closed, which usually means they are breathing. If it does not stay closed, throw away. Wash all of your keepers in fresh water once more before cooking. Keep refrigerated until ready to use.

5. Heat olive oil in sauté pan over medium heat. Sauté garlic and onion until soft, about 1 minute. Add mussels to pan and mix to cover with hot oil. Let cook for about 2 minutes, then deglaze with sherry. Add rosemary sprigs; try to slide them under the mussels into the cooking liquid.

6. Sauté until all the mussels open, about 5-7 minutes. After 7 minutes, if you still have 1 or 2 closed mussels, it's okay to force them open. We throw these out at the restaurant to be extra careful, but at home I would eat them.

7. Add fettuccini to pan and toss. Separate into two serving bowls and enjoy!

T-Bone Fiorentina

I added this recipe to the menu at Paulie's because I wanted to give our guests another meat option that would be a quick pickup for my cooks. I love the T-bone cut because you get both the New York strip and tenderloin in this cut, and it is moderately priced. At Paulie's, we grill to temperature and finish with thyme butter and sea salt flakes. At home, you can sear the T-bone in a cast-iron pan and baste with thyme and butter. Add a bit of black garlic for a special occasion.

Ingredients

- 1 16 oz T-bone
- 4 tbsp unsalted butter
- 1 small bunch fresh thyme
- 2 cloves black garlic, peeled and whole
- Pinch sea salt flakes
- Kosher salt
- Ground black pepper

Directions

1. Heat large pan or cast-iron skillet over medium heat until it reaches temperature, about 4–5 minutes. Add butter, thyme, and garlic.

2. Season both sides of the steak with ground black pepper and kosher salt. Add steak to pan and baste butter on top of steak.

3. Cook on both sides for 2–3 minutes, continuously basting, or until cooked to your liking.

4. Plate the steak and pour remains of pan on top. Sprinkle with sea salt and enjoy!

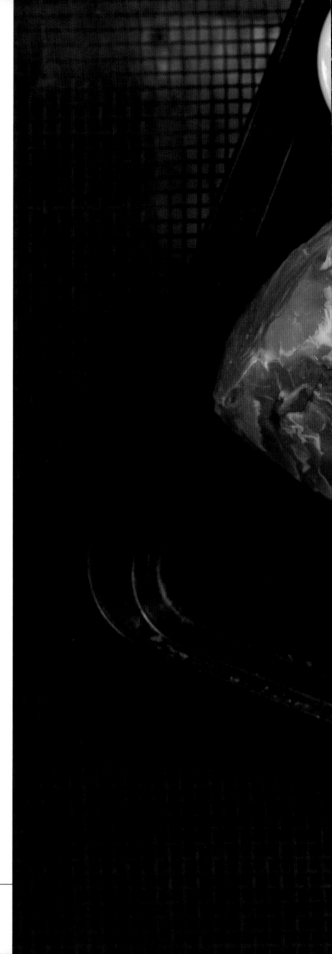

We had wanted the items on our menu to be fresh and made to order. This was great during our first six months, but fresh and made to order was putting us in the shit now. We weighed our options and decided to stick to our philosophy. We rethought the menu to allow quicker pickup times, but everything was made to order as much as possible. Even today, when I add new menu items, in addition to it being fresh, made to order, and delicious, I want it simple and quick to turn around on the line.

It took us quite a while to get used to being crushed on a daily basis. The two sides of a successful restaurant are like this: You have to be busy to succeed, but if you're too busy, the kitchen can't keep up. It's physically and mentally draining. There were days early on when I hoped it would flood so that we could get a break. But we hope that the harder we work, the greater the rewards, and I believe this to be true. My businesses may not make any of us rich, but I take care of my staff the best that I can.

Both of my parents often worked on the line at the same time, or one would work the front while the other was in the kitchen. It wasn't long before I was put in the kitchen too. I wasn't excited about being in the middle of it every day. It was like organized chaos back there, at best, but we did a great job putting out quality product.

Soups were the best. It took so long to get some of the dishes ready that we were constantly behind in those busy days. When someone would order a soup, we'd cheer, ladle it out, and ring for pickup before diving back into the rest.

At Paulie's, we have no expediter and do not take reservations. All you spoiled cooks out there, think about that for a minute. The person that calls out dishes for you—that's your expediter. They read tickets for you and tell each cook station what they have and how many to make. We had to stop what we were doing, pick up the handwritten ticket out of a bowl, read it, put it on the ticket rack, call out items to other cooks, and then go back to our sauté pans. This is not really a big deal for a slow kitchen, but it quickly bogs down a busy kitchen. We wrote tickets by hand until 2013, when I finally installed kitchen printers, one for each side of the kitchen. Hallelujah!

Because we are counter service, we take walk-ins on a first come, first served basis. This means we never know how many covers we will have on any day. There isn't a reservation log to check before dinner service.

After the *Chronicle* review, we could count on being crushed daily, so that's what we prepared for. But we also didn't (and still don't) have the ability to stagger or time the orders that come in. Once a guest

▶ Long time line cooks expediting their own orders.

walks in the door, they want to order quickly and receive their food shortly afterward. So that's our goal every day. Our kitchen is focused on speed. If a cook can't multitask, they can't work for us. We can't afford to waste time. Over the years, we have found that soft cooks don't last very long in our kitchen.

Lower Westheimer has changed a lot since 1998. The caliber of restaurants and bars has improved a great deal. I have seen coffee shops, restaurants, cafes, and bars come and go within the one-mile radius around Paulie's that has now been dubbed "Restaurant Row." The area has even been recognized by national publications, and some of the establishments have been recognized by the James Beard Foundation.

Currently, our neighbors include Hugo's, Underbelly, Anvil, Uchi, Poison Girl, Blacksmith, Southside Espresso, Hay Merchant, One-Fifth, and many others. By the time this book is published, I'm sure there will be more.

Our building went up in the 1950s and has a great vintage look. Lower Westheimer and Montrose have always been high-traffic areas. We were fortunate to find a building we really liked in the area, and we really got lucky with how our immediate area developed.

Paulie's interior is mostly concrete and brick. It was for sale at the time my parents were looking, and my parents put a bid on the building, but they were beaten out by our current landlord. What an investment that would have been!

We've had quite a few family and friends work at Paulie's over the years, and nearly all of them worked for free or in exchange for food. The most memorable was probably my grandfather Frank, not only because we had three generations of Petronella men working together at one time, but because he was hilarious—even though he wasn't trying to be.

Grandpa Frank was hard of hearing, so answering the phone was always an adventure for him. He knew he couldn't hear, but he would still try to answer the phone. He would yell for a bit to the poor soul on the other end and then hand it off to whoever was around. That person then had to implement damage control to the irate customer on the line. Service wasn't our strong suit in the beginning, and it caused some tension during busy lunch shifts, but at the end of the day, these small trials made us laugh and brought us closer together.

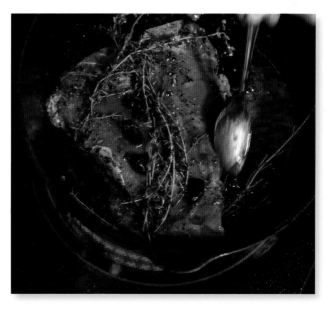

◀ Be sure to constantly baste butter over the meat.

Eggplant Parmigiana

At Paulie's, we prepare individual servings in lasagna boats. At home, you can layer this just like lasagna in a deep baking pan. This has been our Wednesday night special for a very long time. We still have guests who come in every Wednesday night just for this dish. You know who you are, and thank you!

» *Makes about four servings.*

Ingredients

3-4 large standard globe eggplants

3 large eggs

½ cup buttermilk

1 cup seasoned Italian breadcrumbs

1 cup grated Parmesan, extra for sprinkling

2 cups Paulie's Marinara (see page 10)

½ lb low-moisture mozzarella, thinly sliced

3 cups canola frying oil (more or less depending on pan size)

Directions

1. Cut ends off eggplants, peel, and slice longways, about ¼-inch thick.

2. Beat the eggs and buttermilk in large bowl.

3. In another large bowl, combine breadcrumbs and Parmesan. Mix well.

4. In large fry pan, heat oil over medium-high heat, about 360°F. Also, preheat oven to 325°F.

5. Dip eggplant slices into egg mixture, then transfer to breadcrumbs. Cover pieces thoroughly and shake off any excess breadcrumbs before placing into fry oil. Fry on both sides until golden brown. Dark brown and black bits will have a bitter flavor. Remove eggplant from oil and place on paper towels to soak excess oil.

6. In your boats or lasagna pan, lightly cover bottom with small amount of Paulie's Marinara. Cover the marinara with fried eggplant. Follow with another layer of marinara and finish with mozzarella slices. This is one layer. You can layer as high as desired; I would recommend at least two full layers. On your last layer, sprinkle top with Parmesan.

7. Bake about 10-15 minutes, or until cheese is melted. Remove and let cool. Slice and plate. I like to finish with another touch of marinara and more Parmesan.

If that scenario took place at Paulie's today, it would make my skin crawl. I have put so much emphasis on service, and we've worked so hard to cultivate that expectation in our customers, that if someone on my staff had a customer conversation like that, they would most likely be terminated quickly after. So I guess what I'm saying is I would fire my grandfather if he worked at Paulie's today!

Looking back now, those were great moments for me. It's not often that three generations are able to work under the same roof at the same time. I learned how to be tough from those men; that's where I picked up my hard-nosed attitude. I feel like that attitude is what has gotten me through plenty of difficult days at the restaurant. There were days when I wanted to throw up my hands and walk out, but I knew that's not what a Petronella man should do. You tough it out until it passes and then try to learn from the experience. I learned a lot of things the hard way working in Paulie's, but I've tried my best not to repeat my mistakes, and we seem to be doing pretty well.

CHAPTER 4

Career Change

I changed my mind about working in the restaurant after that first summer working there. When I finished college in San Marcos, I returned, armed with a business degree and ready to take over the family business. But I got cold feet.

Shortly after returning to the restaurant, I had a quarter-life crisis. I wasn't sure about running a business at such a young age; I didn't feel I had enough experience. So I decided to put my degree to use in full-service advertising. I started as an unpaid intern, extremely hungry and determined to become a full-time employee. At my first agency, I immediately began planning client media schedules. An unpaid intern planning a multimillion-dollar media campaign is not something the client should ever find out about.

I put in two months of free labor, staying late and asking for more work until I was hired. I soaked up as much as I could at that agency and then moved on to a higher-profile ad agency.

The second agency was where I really got my hands dirty. While there, I was able to become an account executive of a large restaurant account. This is what made me realize I was ready to return to my roots. I realized I could do this on my own. I felt comfortable, confident, and natural making business and marketing decisions for this client.

In hindsight, I learned a great deal, not only about public relations and marketing but also about running a small business. This turned out to be a great experience. I busted my ass and soaked up everything I could in these jobs, and when I was seasoned enough to run my own business, I came back to Paulie's.

My parents teamed up with other family members to open a second location while I was in the advertising world. They knew Paulie's had a decent customer following in the West University-Medical Center area of Houston. There was a vacant Original Pasta Co. at the corner of West Holcombe and Kirby, and when I announced to the family I was ready to return, they offered this location to me. It needed more love and attention than Westheimer, so they gave the grunt work to the kid.

One of the first things I did was plan a trip to Italy. I mapped out an eight-city trip from Milan to Palermo, Sicily. I basically picked eight cities large enough to provide an authentic experience of Italy's different regions. The plan was to find an inspirational restaurant in each city and try to stage—to work for free—for a few days.

▼ The map I used to plan out my Italy destinations!

Because I left home pretty hastily, I didn't contact any of the restaurants before I left. It turns out not too many of them wanted a young American who spoke terrible Italian stumbling around their busy kitchens. So I mostly watched, touched as much as I could, and ate everything. Most of the things I saw weren't far off from what I remembered from my great-grandmother's kitchen.

My first stop was Milan. I wasn't that excited about the food culture in Milan, but I decided to stay one night and walk the city. I wandered to the Duomo Cathedral and through Galleria Vittorio Emanuele II. The cathedral is the second largest in Italy and took six centuries to complete. It also holds the seat of the Archbishop of Milan. The Galleria is a semi-outdoor shopping mall that opens up to the Duomo's front steps, with amazing architecture, of course. The street that houses the Galleria is covered by gorgeous arching glass and a central glass dome. At night, both of these places are gorgeously lit. It was well worth the walk. I grabbed street pizza on the way and took in the sights.

My next stop was Venice, a city that holds my heart and probably always will. As you walk out of the Venice train station, the Santa Lucia, your view is the beautiful Canal Grande. There are no motor vehicles in

▲ 35-mm photos of Venice canals, Rome markets, Boboli Garden, and Sicily fish markets.

Deep-Pan Focaccia

This pizza reminds me of street pizza found in Milan. I like to use active dry yeast with pizza dough. It takes proofing with warm water and sugar beforehand. Most grocery store brands will work fine. I like to find Red Star brand. You will need a deep cake or pie pan for this dough, at least two inches deep.

» *Makes a 10-inch focaccia.*

Ingredients

2 cups 00 flour or Bob's Red Mill bread flour

½ packet active dry yeast (¼-ounce packet)

Pinch kosher salt

Pinch sugar

¼ cup extra virgin olive oil

½ cup hot tap water, not boiling

3 tbsp Paulie's Pesto (see page 44)

6 pitted Kalamata olives, halved

4 thin slices prosciutto

10-inch-wide cake or pie pan, oiled lightly

Directions

1. In small bowl, add hot water to ½ packet of active yeast and sugar, mix, and dissolve well. Let sit at least 10 minutes.

2. In large mixing bowl, add flour and salt. Make a hole in center of flour, then pour in yeast and 1 teaspoon olive oil. Just like making pasta dough, starting in the center, mix a little flour at a time until all is incorporated. Start kneading with your hands for about 10 minutes. You want it elastic with all the flour incorporated. Sticky is okay. If it's too sticky to handle, add flour to your hands. Shape into a neat ball.

3. Cover bowl with plastic or a damp towel; let sit on the counter. Let rise for about 90 minutes. It should double in size.

4. Pop the air bubble and rework into a ball. Place ball on lightly floured workspace and roll into 10-inch circle and then place into baking pan. Cover pan with plastic and let sit another 30 minutes.

5. Preheat oven to 400°F.

6. After 30 minutes, uncover the dough. Push your fingertips into the dough until you feel base of the pan. Do this until you have evenly made dimples all over the dough. Drizzle dough with olive oil so that it pools into the little holes. Cover again with plastic and let rise for another 30 minutes.

7. Remove plastic and spread pesto evenly on the surface. Top with olives and prosciutto. Bake for about 20 minutes or until golden brown. Remove from the oven and let cool before removing focaccia from pan. Slice it up or break it apart. Enjoy!

this part of the city, but you can take a water taxi or gondola to get around. I prefer to walk; you can take in the city more this way.

One of my favorite restaurants in Venice was Trattoria alla Madonna. Although it's in a touristy area, I had a great meal there.

Algiubagio is on the northeast bank of Venice and overlooks the San Michele Cemetery, which was once a prison island and was turned into a burial ground in the 1800s. Even prisons and cemeteries are blanketed by beautiful architecture in Italy.

Osteria L'Orto dei Mori is my personal favorite. I make it a point to dine there every time I visit. The spaghetti nero is my go-to dish. The plate comes dressed in all black—not appealing to most, but I love the resourcefulness. Ink from squid sacs is used to blacken the sauce and add that ocean saltiness.

Osteria Antica Adelaide is a great hole-in-the-wall kind of place that isn't over the top and provides unpretentious local Venetian fare.

My absolute favorite place to be in Venice is the Rialto Market, an open-air fish market that opens at 7:00 a.m., six days a week. It supplies the area with fresh seafood, including whole fish, squid, octopus, prawns, shrimp, and shellfish. By early afternoon, the market is usually sold out and vacant.

After I left Venice, I hopped a two-hour train to Bologna. It's a college town and home of the University of Bologna—the first higher-education institution to use the term university, founded in 1088. Bologna is also the home of great food and restaurants. Ristorante Diana is a gorgeous high-end eatery, one of the many places I aspired to stage. The

▶ My actual itinerary, maps, notes, and photos I brought home.

Spaghetti Nero

This dish is actually much easier to prepare in Italy because fresh squid can be found almost everywhere. Fresh whole squid is much more difficult to find in the United States, unless you are along the coast or have a good fish market in your area. Frozen squid may be easier to find, and you may have to order prepackaged squid ink online. There are European companies that sell packaged squid ink, which I have used plenty.

» *This will serve two.*

Ingredients

1 lb fresh squid, cleaned, tubes and tentacles sliced

8 grams of squid ink

½ lb squid ink spaghetti (see page 137)

¼ cup dry white wine

⅓ cup Paulie's Marinara (see page 10)

Small bunch parsley, minced

2 cloves garlic, sliced

½ yellow onion, chopped

2 tbsp olive oil

Kosher salt

Small pinch red pepper flakes (goes a long way)

Grated pecorino for topping

Directions

1. Bring pot of lightly salted water to boil, drop pasta in, and cook until al dente.

2. In saucepot, heat olive oil over medium heat. Sauté onion and garlic until soft, 2-3 minutes. Season squid with salt and pepper.

3. Deglaze pan with white wine, then add marinara and squid tubes. Save the tentacles for later—tubes are thicker and will need longer to soften. Simmer until tubes are cooked through, about 5 minutes.

4. Add ink, parsley, and tentacles to rest of squid. If you like spice, add pinch of red pepper flakes as well. Mix well and simmer for another few minutes. Sauce should start to thicken now, losing water content, and be completely black!

5. Add spaghetti to sauce and mix well.

6. Separate onto two serving plates and top with grated pecorino. Enjoy!

joke was on me. Literally. The manager chuckled in my face when I asked if I could work for the next two days. But it was an amazing meal and experience nonetheless. Trattoria Battibecco was also an amazing experience—a bit expensive for dinner but affordable for lunch. As grungy as Bologna can be, with college kids bustling around, my dining experiences were high class. I had to make time for the local pescheria (fish market) as well.

Another two-hour train ride took me to Florence a few days later. I did take time to see some of the museums that Florence is known for—Michelangelo's statue of David was much bigger than I expected—but I was there to eat.

Florence is a large city full of great restaurants. Osteria del Porcellino is in the shopping area but very charming, with great service and delicious Tuscan food. The risotto with artichokes and pecorino was killer. Il Latini is a traditional Tuscan restaurant with a great wine cellar. Forno Sartoni was perfect for a quick pizza to go while I was pounding the pavement. But the best dining experience I had in Florence was Enoteca Pinchiorri. This restaurant took traditional Tuscan ingredients and applied modern techniques. It is very beautiful and expensive. You don't see a lot of modern cooking techniques in Italy, so it was refreshing to see it embraced by the community.

While I wandered the city, I trekked out to Boboli Garden, which was gorgeous and meticulously landscaped. I actually took a nap under a tree in the garden.

After Florence came Rome. Like Milan, I wasn't that excited about Rome. There were attractions I wanted to see, but the cuisine didn't excite me. The city was busy and bustling, but I made it to the Vatican, the Colosseum, and the Trevi Fountain. I only caught a few restaurants but spent the most time in Campo di Fiori. During the day, Campo di Fiori is full of market vendors selling seafood, vegetables, clothing, and smallwares. At night, the vendors wrap up, and the surrounding restaurants bring in a vibrant night life.

Another train ride took me to Naples. Pizza was my goal here, and that goal was met. Pizzeria Mattozzi was magical. They've been serving pizza since the mid-1800s. The pizza was amazing, and the service was . . . authentic. By which I mean indifferent. I have met Americans who were disappointed with the service here, but I think it's just what to expect from an Old World Italian place. It's like going to Chinatown in Houston: You're not going for the service; you're going for the food.

Pizzeria Brandi was worth the trip. It is believed to be the oldest pizzeria in Naples, so it can be a tourist destination.

But the best pizza, in my opinion, was L'Antica Pizzeria da Michele—great flavor, a nice ratio of ingredients, acidic sauce. I was a fan.

The longest train ride of the trip was Naples to Messina, Sicily, coming in at about six hours. The most interesting part of the train ride was how the train reached the island of Sicily. The cars pull onto a ferry, the passengers stay in their seats, and the train cars reconnect to the tracks as the ferry docks in Messina.

I didn't do much sightseeing in Messina, although I did see a lot of old men sitting outside, playing cards, and sipping espresso or alcohol. It reminded me of my great-grandfather and the simple pleasures.

Palermo was a great experience. My family is from Sicily—more specifically, Corleone, which is about thirty

minutes from Palermo. I visited all the open-air markets I could find in Palermo. The largest is the Vucciria market. It spans several streets. From what I can tell, it supplies most of the city with everyday needs: seafood, pasta, produce, bathroom necessities, clothing, shoes, artifacts—anything the locals need on a daily basis. I also found the Mercato del Capo, another market that supplies tons of fresh seafood. Looking at whole swordfish on ice was breathtaking; I could tell a few steaks had been cut out of the carcasses already.

While there, I made time to eat and study at Osteria dei Vespri. It was an unassuming family-owned restaurant that served fresh Sicilian ingredients with a pretty interesting wine list. It was nothing overboard, just simple, homey, and delicious—the essence of family-owned Sicilian restaurants.

When I returned home, I was equipped with a camera full of images, a book full of notes and memories, and a desire to change the world.

To build more traffic and potentially bring in a younger crowd at the new Paulie's location, I composed menus of my own during slow days. They were authentic Italian dishes, usually four or five courses, including dessert. The challenge with this location was pumping a new energy into an already-established concept without changing the concept. I had to be careful not to change the menu too much to avoid scaring off our loyal customer base, while still making it sharper. Most times, this is more difficult than opening a new restaurant from scratch.

Neapolitan Margherita Pizza

I like to use active dry yeast to make pizza dough. It takes proofing with warm water and sugar beforehand. Most grocery store brands will work fine, but I like to find Red Star. You will probably want to pick up a pizza stone for your home. It helps the bottom of the pie cook faster and more evenly.

» *Makes two medium thin-crust pizzas.*

Ingredients

½ packet active dry yeast (¼-ounce packet)

Pinch of sugar

½ cup hot tap water, not boiling

2 cups 00 flour, or Bob's Red Mill bread flour

Pinch of kosher salt

1 tsp olive oil

1 ball fresh mozzarella, ovoline

8–10 grape tomatoes, cut in half

6 fresh basil leaves, torn roughly

½ cup Paulie's Marinara (see page 10)

Ground black pepper

Pizza stone

Directions

1. In small bowl, add hot water to ½ packet of active yeast and sugar, mix, and dissolve well. Let sit at least 10 minutes.

2. In large mixing bowl, add flour and salt. Make a hole in center of flour, then pour in yeast and olive oil. Just like making pasta dough, starting in the center, mix a little flour at a time until all is incorporated. Knead with your hands for about 10 minutes. You want it elastic with all the flour incorporated. Sticky is okay. If it's too sticky to handle, add flour to your hands. Shape into a neat ball.

3. Cover bowl with plastic or a damp towel and let sit on the counter. Let rise for about 90 minutes; it should double in size.

4. Pop the air bubble and divide into 2 balls. Place balls on parchment paper or lightly floured foil, make space between, and cover loosely with plastic. Let rise again for another 90 minutes.

5. Preheat oven to 425°F. Let pizza stone heat for at least 30 minutes at 425°F. A pizza stone is the closest we will get to Neapolitan pizza in the home kitchen. The wood-fired ovens that sizzle to 900°F are truly the greatest and the trick to crispy thin crust in less than 5 minutes.

6. Pop any air bubbles in the dough ball. Lightly flour a working surface. If you want thin pizza, pull the dough until it is translucent. It will want to spring back, so continue to push out dough with your hands until desired thickness. Throwing it back and forth between your hands is a good way to stretch the dough without flattening it. You can use a rolling pin in the beginning, but too much rolling will squeeze out the air, leaving the dough dense. By pushing out the edges of the dough, make a crust. Pinch a hump around the edges. Continue pushing out the dough from the edges until you are happy with the size. You can throw it in the air toward a light to check for translucence. Tossing in the air also helps in stretching without losing fluffiness.

7. Place dough on lightly floured pizza peel before adding toppings. Spoon marinara across dough, leaving ½ inch around the edges. Add halved grape tomatoes. Season tomatoes with salt and pepper. Slide pizza onto pizza stone. Let bake for about 5 minutes. Cut the fresh mozzarella into thin, small pieces. Because fresh mozzarella carries water, place pieces on paper towel beforehand to reduce water content. Place mozzarella on pizza, leaving about 2 inches around edges.

8. Bake for another 10-15 minutes. You will see the dough start to bubble and crust. Remove when browned on bottom and around edges. Finish with fresh basil leaves. *Mangia!*

Here are some other of my favorite topping combinations:

*Marinara, shredded mozzarella, anchovy fillets, sautéed onions, and mushrooms

*Marinara, pepperoni, fresh oregano, feta cheese

▶ Marinara, pepperoni, fresh oregano and feta.

▶ Marinara, shredded mozzarella, anchovy, sautéed onions, and mushrooms.

▼ Pizza dough steps illustrated, from mixing to kneading to rolling

Tortellini in Brodo

I love making this dish in the winter, or anytime I buy a whole chicken. I simply heat up the brodo, add a squeeze of lemon juice, and drink it from a coffee cup. One whole chicken, some flour, and eggs can produce an everlasting meal. This is a very popular dish in Bologna. There are many variations, depending on what's available for the filling and your taste preference. My variation is simple, classic, and flavorful. I like to garnish with mint at the end; it adds a bit of freshness to the brodo.

For the Brodo

1 whole chicken with giblets

8 qt water

Kosher salt

Small bunch aromatics of your choice (I prefer thyme, sage, and rosemary)

3 bay leaves

6 cloves garlic, peeled, whole

Whole peppercorns, handful

3 celery stalks, cleaned, chopped

3 carrots, peeled, chopped

1 yellow onion, chopped

For the Tortellini

¼ lb ground pork sausage, seasoned

2 oz ricotta

1 tbsp grated Parmesan

Ground black pepper

Fresh mint, for garnish

1 batch egg pasta dough (see page 137)

Directions for Brodo

1. Start to simmer the water over medium heat in large stockpot; add ¼ cup kosher salt.

2. While waiting for water to simmer, break down your chicken. I actually love breaking down chickens; it's really easy and produces lots of fruits of labor. This chicken will give us a stock, two chicken breasts, two thighs, and two legs. We're going to add the wings to the stock. Chicken stock is valuable in the kitchen. We use it in risotto and many other dishes as well. (Note: I'm not going to describe breaking down a chicken. There are plenty of really good videos on YouTube that are much easier to follow. Once you do it the first time, you will get the hang of it. Keep the breasts, thighs, and legs for future use—such as tomorrow night's dinner. Add everything else to the stockpot: giblets, backbone, wings, and any unwanted skin and bones.)

3. Add the aromatics, garlic, peppercorns, celery, carrots, and onion. Continue to bring to simmer. Once bubbling begins, lower heat to low. You never want an aggressive boil. Simmer for 3 hours, scooping any foam from the top throughout, which are impurities.

4. When done, turn off heat and let cool. Your house should smell amazing. Using a slotted spoon, scoop out the large items. I actually like to eat some of the delicious soft vegetables. Strain the stock through a fine strainer. Then strain again in cheesecloth, or coffee filters if you'd like to be resourceful. It's important the brodo be clear of debris. Brodo keeps well for a few days refrigerated or a few weeks frozen.

Directions for Tortellini

1. In small bowl, mix pork, ricotta, 1 tbsp grated Parmesan, and ground black pepper. Mix well until all ingredients are incorporated and filling is uniform.

2. Pinch off ¼ ball of dough. Roll pasta dough through pasta roller on #6 setting. Lay out on dry, floured surface or parchment paper. With cutter wheel, cut out 1½-inch squares. Place dime-size filling in the center of each square. Have a small bowl of water to dip fingers in. Wet the inside of all four sides. Pinch two opposite corners together to form a triangle. Make sure they are moist and stay together. Close up one side, and then push out any air before closing up the other side. Again, make sure fingers are moist and pasta stays closed. Now, you want to pinch the two outside corners together. Fold the corners over your index finger to make a ring. Place on dry sheet pan, lightly floured, with space between each other; 6–7 tortellini per person is sufficient.

3. When ready to make the tortellini in brodo, bring pot of water to boil and salt lightly. In another pot, bring brodo to simmer, about 2 cups per person. Drop the tortellini in the boiling water for 2 minutes. Try not to cook too many at a time; you want to give them enough space to roam.

4. Ladle hot brodo into a serving bowl. With slotted spoon, remove tortellini and place in brodo. Garnish with fresh mint leaves. Enjoy!

Zuppa di Fagioli

This soup is a Tuscan favorite. There are many different ways to prepare it, but this dish always features white beans, or cannellini beans. My great-grandmother would have simply added a chicken broth, soffritto, and garlic and served it with rustic bread. I'm going to spruce it up a bit.

» *Makes about four servings.*

Ingredients

- 1 cup dry white beans (cannellini, great northern, or navy beans)
- 2 cups chicken broth (see page 106)
- 3 large fresh tomatoes, diced
- 3 oz pancetta, diced
- ½ yellow onion, diced
- 1 carrot, peeled, diced
- 2 stalks celery, cleaned, diced
- 2 cloves garlic, diced
- 3 tbsp extra virgin olive oil
- 1 large sprig rosemary
- 2 bay leaves
- Kosher salt
- Ground black pepper
- 1 loaf rustic Italian bread

Directions

1. Soak the beans in water overnight. Drain off water and bring to boil in lightly salted fresh water. Cook for about 15 minutes. Drain and set aside.

2. Combine garlic, celery, carrot, onion, and pancetta. In large soup pot, heat the olive oil and sauté this mix with rosemary and bay leaves. Sauté until veggies soften and pancetta browns.

3. Add the beans and mix well, marrying everything together. Add broth and tomatoes and season with salt and pepper. Mix well, cover the pot, and heat over low heat for about 30–45 minutes, or until beans are tender but not mushy. When ready, remove rosemary sprig and bay leaves.

4. Ladle soup into bowls and top with bread. Bread can be used to soak up the delicious juices.

◀ Caffè corretto: Espresso with grappa. Reminds me of old men in Sicily.

I decided to try my own pop-up. A pop-up is when a restaurant invites local chefs to use their space for a night, but I wanted to use my own kitchen to experiment. I announced the pop-ups through an email blast and took reservations through replies to the email. I put together a few tables in the back of the restaurant and served family style while the rest of the restaurant ran our normal menu. I was cooking on both sides, putting out food for the pop-up and helping on the line if we got busy.

I really enjoyed the experiment. It was a chance to exercise my creative side with food that inspired me. When I think back now, I'm surprised people actually showed up to these dinners! I had no name recognition and no professional cooking experience. I only knew what my family had taught me and what I learned from years of being in the kitchen. I'm really grateful to those who trusted me.

In those days, I was wearing several hats as general manager, operator, and line cook. I had to choose the employees I could trust with responsibility and demote those I could not trust. I inherited some pretty interesting characters. This position challenged my management and delegating abilities, but I had always been a doer, so I put my head down and did what it took to get the job done.

After two years of trying to pump new energy into this location, we were approached by another restaurant operator, who wanted the space for their own concept. We had not put the space on the market, and I was still 100 percent invested with my time. But I talked over the offer with the family, and we decided it could actually be a good thing. Although I was all-in with this location, the location never felt like a great fit. It was different from the original on Westheimer, and we all felt it.

▼ Pears roasted in sherry, allspice, and honey.

Limoncello

Citrus orchards are bountiful in Sicily and southern Italy. When Italy gives you lemons, you make limoncello. I love this liqueur after dinner; it's sweet enough to satisfy my sweet tooth, and the alcohol helps digestion. It's also very satisfying to drink from your own personal batch. It takes some time, so be patient. After your first batch, you will know if you like less sweet, or less alcohol, etc. Please, make this recipe your own.

Directions

1. Combine zest of 15 lemons with 750 ml bottle of Everclear, or 190-proof grain alcohol. Wash lemons well with warm water and scrubber. Make sure you are zesting the yellow skin only, as the white pith will create a bitter taste. Sanitize a jar or bottle big enough to hold both alcohol and zest.

2. Date the bottle and let sit 10 days, shaking every day.

3. Put away for 60 days.

4. Bring 5 cups of water to a boil, remove from heat, and add 2.5 cups of sugar. Stir well, dissolving all sugar, and let cool.

5. Add to alcohol and let sit another 60 days.

6. Filter liqueur well through cheesecloth. You don't want any bits or residue.

7. Bottle your new liqueur and let sit a week before tasting.

I also like to make grapefruit-cello, or pompelmocello. Substitute 9 large grapefruit and 3.5 cups sugar.

Cacio e Pepe

As simple as this dish sounds, to master it takes practice and technique. So if you're not happy in the beginning, keep practicing! I like to use spaghetti here, but bucatini or another long pasta will work too. This dish is a prime example of Italian cooking, using what you have in the pantry and making it delicious.

» *This will serve two.*

Ingredients

½ lb spaghetti (see page 137)

2 tbsp unsalted butter

1 tbsp cracked black pepper

Kosher salt

½ cup grated Parmesan

¼ cup grated pecorino

Directions

1. Bring pot of lightly salted water to boil. Drop in pasta. Cook until al dente. Save about ¾ cup of pasta water.

2. In sauté pan over medium-low heat, add 1 tablespoon butter and 1 tablespoon freshly cracked black pepper. Sauté pepper in butter for about 1 minute. You want to smell the pepper coming out of the pan.

3. Add pasta and about ¼ cup of pasta water to pan. Mix well. Immediately, add 1 tablespoon butter and half the cheeses. Toss continuously to prevent sticking. Add remaining cheese and a little pasta water. You want the cheese to melt to a creamy texture, no more than 2 minutes. If it gets too dry, add a bit more pasta water until creaminess comes back.

4. Separate into two serving bowls. Top with freshly ground pepper and more cheese if desired.

Rosemary Scallops

This dish was one of my pop-up ideas back in 2007. It has since become unoriginal, but it's still pretty cool and delicious . . . and super easy at home. The rosemary infuses the scallops from the inside out, and the crispy garlic bits are delicious to me. These are great as antipasti.

Ingredients

9 large sea scallops

3 large rosemary sprigs, strong enough to hold 3 scallops each

Juice of 1 lemon

2 tbsp extra virgin olive oil

1 tsp kosher salt

1 tsp cracked black pepper

2 garlic cloves, minced

Fresh fennel fronds

Directions

1. In a small mixing bowl, mix lemon juice, garlic, salt, and pepper. Toss in scallops and dress evenly.

2. Peel off rosemary leaves, starting from the bottom to about an inch from the top. Whittle the base of the skewer to a fine point. Slide 3 dressed scallops onto each skewer.

3. Heat olive oil in sauté pan over medium-high heat. Add scallops and sauté on both sides for about 3–4 minutes. You are looking for a light golden brown coloration on each side.

4. Place scallops on serving plate and garnish with fennel fronds. You may want to remove from skewers before passing to guests.

Fresh Fruit Salad

This fruit salad is a bit different than Paulie's version. It is super easy and can easily be substituted with different fruits. Here, I'm using my favorite combinations. You have to remember I am an acid freak; try it with lemon juice first. You may feel it is too acidic.

» *This serves one.*

Ingredients

10–12 red grapes

2 kiwi

1 blood orange

Juice of ½ lemon

Sea salt

4–5 mint leaves, chiffonade

Directions

1. Wash the grapes well and slice in half. Peel and slice the kiwis. Peel and separate orange segments.

2. Combine fruit, mint leaves, and fresh lemon juice in bowl. Lightly sprinkle sea salt and enjoy!

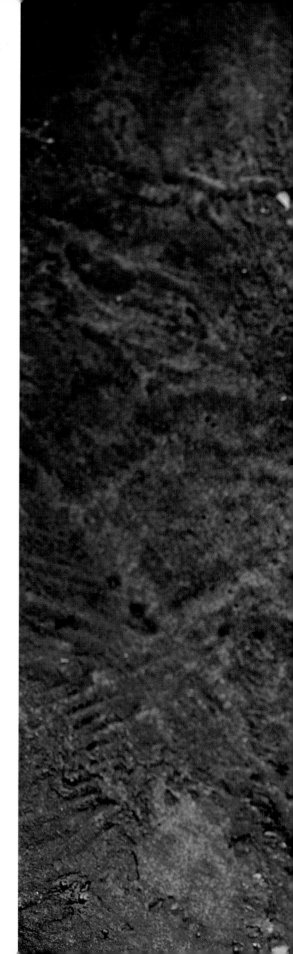

Citrus Asparagus

This definitely reminds me of Italy. If I can find asparagus, it usually shows up on my Thanksgiving dinner menu at home. It's easy to make and involves fresh, vibrant flavors.

» *This will serve three to four as a side dish.*

Ingredients

- 1 lb jumbo asparagus, roughly all same size
- Zest and juice of 1 lemon
- Zest and segments of 1 orange
- 1 tsp fresh oregano
- 2 mint sprigs, leaves chiffonade
- 1 garlic clove, minced
- ¼ cup extra virgin olive oil
- Ground black pepper
- Kosher salt
- Sea salt

Directions

1. Bring pot of water to boil and salt lightly with kosher salt. Cut off tough ends of asparagus, trying to leave them all the same length.

2. Cook asparagus until tender to your liking, about 2 minutes. Remove and add to ice bath to stop cooking. Once cooled, about 4–5 minutes, pat dry and transfer to large mixing bowl.

3. Add lemon zest, lemon juice, orange zest, orange segments, oregano, mint, garlic, olive oil, and ground black pepper. Toss well, then place spears on serving plate. Pour mixture over spears and sprinkle sea salt. Serve family style.

Roasted Pears and Chocolate

This is one of my favorite desserts ever. I have seen it prepared a few different ways; below is a combination of my favorite techniques and ingredients. It requires a bit of baking experience but is fairly simple. I love pears and I love chocolate. Win–win!

» *This serves four.*

Ingredients

- 4 pears, best available in your area will work
- ½ tsp ground allspice
- 1 cup dry sherry
- ¼ cup honey
- 3 tbsp unsalted butter
- 2 eggs
- 1 tbsp powdered sugar
- 4 ounces semisweet chocolate chips
- 1 cup water

Directions

1. Preheat oven to 375°F. You will need a large sauté pan or skillet.

2. Peel the pears, but leave the stem to help in transferring later. Also, slice bottom of pear so that it can stand upright.

3. Place pears in pan, add sherry and water, and bake for 30-40 minutes, checking for tenderness. Make sure to baste the pears throughout baking process.

4. Place baked pears on a plate. Pour pan juices in mixing bowl. Add allspice and honey to bowl and whisk thoroughly until all is incorporated.

5. Place pears back into pan, pour mixture over all pears evenly, and bake another 5-7 minutes. Continue to baste. Remove pan and set aside to cool.

6. In a double boiler, stir together butter and chocolate chips until melted. If you don't have a double boiler, you can use a stainless mixing bowl over a hot pot of water. Make sure water never gets into chocolate.

7. Separate your eggs. Remove chocolate from double boiler and whisk in egg yolks. In another bowl, whisk egg whites and powdered sugar. You can use a hand mixer here, as you will need stiff peaks. Fold egg-white mixture into chocolate mixture. You basically made chocolate royal icing.

8. Place pears on serving plates, drizzle generously with chocolate, and serve. Fork and knife recommended. Enjoy!

CHAPTER 5

Back to Basics

Selling the Holcombe location and moving to the Westheimer location full-time allowed my parents to remove themselves. This location was operationally stronger than Holcombe, but it needed new life as well. Although it wasn't necessarily broken, it also wasn't accelerating—just kind of coasting. When a business coasts too long, complacency soon follows. We had a very loyal customer base, which was a great sign, but I wanted to grow.

The existing customer culture at Paulie's did not allow for a large menu change, so one of the ways I satisfied my personal creative side was providing the restaurant space to other young chefs trying to find their voice, living vicariously through these guys and gals. We are closed on Sundays, so I opened my door to chefs to operate their own pop-up dinners, with their food, their staff, their food costs, their price points. The only money I kept was to recoup my own food costs or to tip out my staff who may have helped.

One of the first chefs to use our kitchen was Randy Rucker, right as he was in full stride with his *tenacity* dinners. Rucker is one of the most creative chefs I have been around, and I'm glad to call him a close friend. We have known each other since middle school. Rucker has been in our kitchen several times—probably the most of any of the pop-up chefs.

On October 10, 2010, Seth Siegel-Gardner (from The Pass & Provisions, in Houston), Justin Yu (from Oxheart, in Houston), and Willet Feng (also from Oxheart) coordinated the unforgettable "10-10-10" dinner. Coffee guru David Buehrer (from Greenway Coffee Co., in Houston) was on hand to pair beverages.

I had not planned to attend the dinner (I had a friend's wedding to attend), but felt the need to stop in and check on things. The front of the house was in the weeds when I showed up. It was so bad that we had to visit each table and ask them what course they were on. That was a little embarrassing with the *Houston Chronicle* food writer in the house.

But that's why we have pop-ups. They are not meant to be perfect; they prepare young professionals for a real restaurant experience. I always appreciate customers who attend experimental pop-ups, because they really are subjecting themselves as guinea pigs.

Some of the other talented cooks who have graced the Paulie's kitchen are Chris Shepherd (from Underbelly, in Houston), Terrence Gallivan (from The Pass & Provisions), Justin Basye (from Pappas Restaurant Group, in Houston), Michael Gaspard (also from Pappas Restaurant Group), Ned Elliott (from Foreign & Domestic, in Austin), Chris Leung (from Cloud 10 Creamery, in Houston), and Ronnie Killen (from Killen's, in Pearland).

All of these chefs are celebrating their own success today. We continue to open our doors on Sundays to those who would like to run their own menus.

One of the first things I did when taking over Westheimer was cook on the line every day. I believe the kitchen is the engine room of a restaurant, so I knew I had to start there. We had several longtime cooks, but they had been on cruise control for a while. I wanted them to pay attention to the details and take ownership of their plates, so I put my whites on and went to work. If the kitchen staff was truly going to respect the son taking over, I had to show them I was ready to join the fray. I had to show them I was just as diligent and fast as they were.

I was one of four cooks, I was never the fastest, but I was the most meticulous. Our kitchen is so hectic that you have to be working and thinking about five things at once—not to mention the constant specter of my operational responsibilities. If I was tired or hungover or sick that day, it showed.

I worked the line for lunch, then, on my break, I would take inventory and order goods or pay invoices or attend to a maintenance issue, shove food in my face, and get back on the line for dinner. I did this six days a week for three or four years. It was mentally and physically taxing, but I am glad I did it. I found out who was on my side and who wasn't. It made our kitchen bond stronger.

After a few years, I realized this wasn't the best place to keep spending my time. I had to start growing

▲ Many talented chefs have graced the Paulie's kitchen on Sundays, including Ned Elliott, Mark Clayton, Chris Leung, Randy Rucker, and Nathan Lemley.

FOREIGN & DOMESTIC
CHRISTMAS EVE 2011
FEAST OF THE 7 FISHES

ANTIPASTO
MEATS, PICKLES, MUSTARD, JAM, BRIOCHE

1ST COURSE
SQUID
LEMON, OREGANO, PAPRIKA

the rest of the business. I had to focus on the front of house and overall operations.

Much like the front of house I inherited at the Holcombe location, Westheimer didn't have the friendliest staff. As I was working the line twice a day, I was also interviewing barista applicants between shifts. I interviewed so many front-of-house applicants from 2009 to 2013 that I was exhausted. It was a challenge convincing talented people they could make money at a counter-service restaurant, but I didn't believe that because we were counter service we had to settle for less than excellent customer service. I knew that I had to give them a trade or incentivize them more.

Changing the coffee program did exactly that. Installing a high-integrity coffee program attracted a higher-integrity employee and brought in new customers, killing two birds with one stone. I was going to make every counter-service employee a trained barista. I wanted the friendly coffee aficionado who was interested in becoming a professional.

And that's what it did. We proved you could make a decent living while working the counter at Paulie's. I teamed up with David Buehrer and Greenway Coffee to organize coffee training for every new hire. Every new hire for the front of house had to go through a week of training at Greenway Coffee Company before they could work on the floor at Paulie's.

We were also now serving SCAA (Specialty Coffee Association of America)–style coffee, and it was amazing. The focus on coffee in restaurants is often put on the back burner, so to speak. Many restaurants focus on food, wine, or cocktails, but they rarely practice the same integrity with coffee. Yet coffee is often the last thing that hits your palate at a restaurant.

Paulie's Coffee Protocol

Espresso Drinks

Espresso

17-23g of coffee grinds

Brew time between 25-30 sec

Wet weight of 27-34g

Finished when it looks like warm honey

Cappuccino

2 shots of espresso

Steamed and textured milk

Served in 6 oz cup

Latte

2 shots espresso

Steamed and textured milk

Served in 12 oz cups

Macchiato

1 shot of espresso

1 oz steamed and textured milk

1 shot of espresso side car

Served in espresso cup

Americano

2 shots espresso

5 oz hot water

Served in 6 oz cup

Chemex

30 grams coffee

500 grams water

Bloom for 45 seconds

Brew time between 3:30 and 4:00

Milk Steaming

1. Purge steaming wand

2. Steam and texture milk

3. Clean and purge steaming wand

 Paulie's serves locally roasted coffee from Greenway coffee

All coffee drinks are served on matching saucers with a demitasse spoon.

Continued

How to Make Espresso Step by Step

1. Unlatch the portafilter.
2. Knock out the old grounds if the previous person did not.
3. Wipe the portafilter basket clean and dry. Ensure all basket holes are clear.
4. Turn on the grinder.
5. Begin dosing. Rotate the portafilter while dosing to distribute the grounds evenly throughout the basket as it fills.
6. Turn off the grinder when you estimate the proper amount has been ground.
7. Finish dosing.
8. Groom the dose.
9. Be sure the tamper is dry and free of grounds.
10. Tamp lightly (about 30 lbs).
11. Wipe any loose grounds from the rim of the portafilter basket.
12. Flush the machine.
13. Latch on the portafilter and engage the pump.
14. Observe the underside of the portafilter. If there is immediate channeling, consider the possible cause, address it, and return to step 1. (This usually applies when using a bottomless or naked portafilter.)
15. Stop the flow based on your desired shot volume or color.
16. Serve the shot immediately.
17. If the flow rate was faster or slower than desired, consider whether to adjust the grind.

Cleaning the Machines

Espresso Machine Cleaning

1. Unscrew screen from group head.
2. Remove filter from portafilter and soak in coffee cleaning solution with the group head screens.
3. Put 1 scoop of coffee cleaner in both blank portafilters.
4. Turn on machine for 10 seconds and turn off machine for 10 seconds.
5. Repeat step 4 six times.
6. Dump out excess water.
7. Repeat step 5 without coffee cleaner three times.
8. Scrub portafilters, screens, and filters.
9. Replace parts.
10. Empty knock box and rinse it out.
11. Rinse out drip pan.
12. Dump drain bucket outside, and rinse it out before returning it to the machine.
13. Make sure both drain hoses are put back in the drain bucket.

Nightly Grinder Cleaning

1. Clear beans out of grinder.
2. Put beans from hopper into coffee bags.
3. Brush out and vacuum inside of the grinder.
4. Wipe out hoppers with a dry rag or paper towel.
5. Return hoppers to the grinders.
6. Wipe down outside of grinder.
7. Rinse and wipe down pitcher rinse station and underneath it as well.

▶ Red is our favorite color at Paulie's.

HAND POUR	3.00
ESPRESSO	2.50
AMERICANO	2.50
MACCHIATO	2.75
CAPPUCCINO	3.00
CORTADO	3.00

Friday Night Grinder Cleaning

1. Take apart machine.
2. Unscrew grinding burrs and remove springs.
3. Vacuum and brush out machine.
4. Put machine back together.
5. CHECK THE THREADING ON THE COLLAR.

Cleaning Chemex

Always hand wash glass equipment.
Rinse out chemex with coffee cleaning solution, and dry with paper towel every night.

Coffee Cleaning Solution

1 scoop of cleaner per 2 cups of **HOT** water

Job Description and Duties

Morning Coffee Duties

- Set grinder.
- Check espresso by tasting.
- Make sure you have 3 towels: 1 for drying the portafilter, 1 for cleaning the steaming wand, and 1 sanitary towel.
- At the end of your shift, dump out knock box and drain bucket. Also, back flush (no cleaner) both group heads at the SAME time. After, brush them gently and wipe them out with a rag. Make sure the steam wands are clean and free of hardened milk. Essentially, you are hitting the restart button for the next shift.
- Once a week, deep clean and wipe down entire coffee area, including taking cups off of the top of the machine and wiping it down.

Night Barista

- Make sure you have 3 clean towels at the start of your shift.
- Double check that the previous shift did what they were supposed to do.
- Clean grinder.
- Clean machine.
- Wipe down counter.
- Put all dirty towels in the hamper.
- Dump out knock box and drain bucket.

Latte pouring.

I'll never forget this transition period. I received blowback from customers about the wait times to make fresh coffee instead of serving old, burnt coffee that had been sitting in hot pots for hours. A particular older man felt compelled to yell at me through the kitchen as I was cooking on the line, "I just want black coffee right now! You're going to fail, idiot!"

The majority of Paulie's sales is food; our coffee sales make up only 2 percent of the total receipts. Besides making coffee, our baristas spend most of their time taking orders, attending to customers, or pushing food out. So, to keep them sharp on their coffee skills, I curate a latté art tournament every March during March Madness basketball season. I draw up a bracket and pit every barista against one another to make the most perfect latté art. Sure, latté art looks beautiful on top of an espresso drink, but there is talent behind it and a purpose: A beautiful design is a seal of approval that the milk was textured and steamed properly. If the milk does not separate clearly from the espresso, it means skill was lacking while steaming the milk.

> **"You cannot make a perfect drink with imperfect ingredients."**

The tournament lasts almost two months. Each barista has an entire week to practice their skills and send me a picture of their best effort. The winner moves on to the next round, the tournament is double elimination, so everyone gets a second chance. The champion wins a round-trip flight to anywhere they want to go. Because I purchase everything I can at the restaurant with a credit card, I accumulate tons of travel miles, so I transfer a ticket in their name. The second-place winner usually receives an iPad, and third place receives a home coffee-brewing kit. I believe a healthy competition breeds excellence.

You cannot make a perfect drink with imperfect ingredients. There are three components to great coffee: the barista, the equipment, and the roasted beans. We do our best to excel with all three.

In addition to creating the coffee program, I started making the majority of our pasta in-house. I purchased a pasta-extruding machine and asked Seth Siegel-Gardner and Terrence Gallivan (from The Pass & Provisions, in Houston) to play with the machine and come up with new recipes for our menu. I really understood the idea of delegating at this point.

Handmade pasta is one of the most satisfying foods to make by hand. You get to watch very simple ingredients come together to form a magical substance. It is something kids can enjoy with their family, too. I remember covering my hands in dough when I cooked with my great-grandmother. It is a process that is relaxing and satisfying.

Egg Pasta Dough

» *Yields about 4 lb fresh pasta, or 15–20 large ravioli, agnolotti, tortellini, etc.*

» *You may subsitute dry pasta for any of the pasta recipes in this book.*

Ingredients

3 large eggs

2 cups Bob's Red Mill
    all-purpose flour

Pinch of kosher salt

1 tbsp olive oil

*Black Pasta Dough

3 packs squid ink
    (4 grams each)

Directions

For home cooking, I like to use Bob's Red Mill all-purpose flour. Most supermarkets carry this. He offers several different types of flour made from quality product, including gluten-free. Super-fine 00 flour is my favorite, but a little harder to find for the home cook. All-purpose flour will work fine at home.

You may start your pasta dough on a clean and dry wood or marble surface. I like to use an oversize stainless or glass mixing bowl. This helps with mess and keeps all ingredients in one place.

1. Make a hole in the center of your flour mound; sprinkle the salt around your flour. Beat the eggs and oil with a fork in the center. (Add squid ink here, if making black pasta.)

2. Slowly incorporate more and more flour into your center as you're mixing. When your flour is incorporated, use your hands to knead the dough for about 10 minutes. If it gets sticky, sprinkle with more flour. If it gets too dry, add a bit of water to your hands. If you are making dough to eat immediately, cover the bowl with a dry kitchen towel and let sit for 30 minutes. If you are making for later use, wrap dough tightly in plastic wrap and refrigerate until ready. Invest in a KitchenAid pasta roller attachment. It guarantees consistent thickness. There is a hand-roll model as well, but the automatic attachment allows you to free both hands, which you will need.

3. Make room on either your counter or long baking sheets to place your rolled dough. Make sure surface is covered with flour; you don't want your dough sticking. Tear off about ¼ of the dough ball, flatten with your hands, and run through setting #1 five or six times. Fold it in thirds each time. Run dough through setting #2 once, #3 once, #4 once, and finally #5 once. By this time, dough should be about 2 feet long. You can either run through the spaghetti or fettuccini attachment also available for KitchenAid or lay out for ravioli, agnolotti, or tortellini (stuffed pasta). Run through #6 for stuffed pasta dough. Always have flour lying around to sprinkle work area and dough.

The problem I had with making pasta by hand at the restaurant was time. Hand-rolling and -cutting enough pasta for our volume would take all day, maybe the night before as well. It wasn't efficient enough for what I needed, so I looked into the company Arcobaleno, which I was introduced to by the StarChefs Congress in New York. They make several sizes of dough mixers and extruders. I started with a tabletop model and quickly grew out of it. The extruder we have now is capable of mixing our semolina flour and water in a hopper, then extruding it out of specifically cut dies to create several different pasta shapes. We make everything we need for two days in about two hours. And we sell a lot of pasta, somewhere around 100–200 pounds every day. We have also made pasta for a few neighboring restaurants in Houston, including Roost, Underbelly, and Monarch at the Zaza Hotel.

One sector of the business that I did not want to change was the desserts. Paulie's has been known for decorated shortbread cookies since before we existed. (My stepmother, Kathy, started them at a catering business prior to opening Paulie's.) The shortbread cookies at Paulie's come in many different shapes, mostly coordinating with the time of year or holiday, including Valentine's Day, Easter, Mother's Day, Father's Day, rodeo season, Halloween, Thanksgiving, and especially Christmas. We make about ten thousand shortbread cookies during December for Christmas orders.

Our other popular desserts include chocolate chip cookies, which we also serve at the OKRA Charity Saloon, baked to order (OKRA stands for Organized Kollaboration on Restaurant Affairs). This way, they arrive still hot and gooey, kinda falling apart—my favorite way to eat chocolate chip cookies. An order may take fifteen minutes to arrive, but it's well worth it when they arrive with a cold glass of milk.

Paulie's also makes amazing oatmeal raisin cookies, raspberry linzers, cream cheese brownies, key lime tarts, mini chocolate fudge cakes, bread pudding with amaretto sauce (made from leftover panini bread), and peanut butter cookies dipped in dark chocolate.

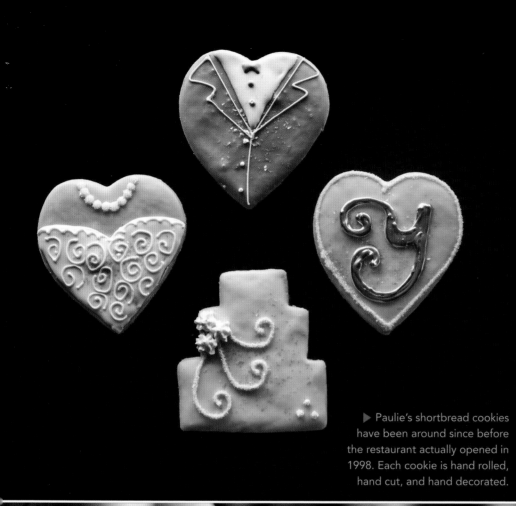

▶ Paulie's shortbread cookies have been around since before the restaurant actually opened in 1998. Each cookie is hand rolled, hand cut, and hand decorated.

Cream Cheese Brownies

These suckers are decadent and rich! At Paulie's, we drizzle with white chocolate for added presentation. This recipe has been decreased from our batch amounts, but still makes a good deal of brownies.

» *This recipe should be enough for a small pan. Measurements are by weight.*

Ingredients for Brownie Batter

1 lb semisweet chocolate chips

6 oz unsalted butter

12 oz Bob's Red Mill all-purpose flour

1 tbsp baking powder

1 tsp salt

24 oz granulated sugar

8 eggs

1 tbsp vanilla extract

Cream Cheese Filling

1 lb cream cheese, room temp

3 oz unsalted butter, room temp

3 eggs

5 oz granulated sugar

1 tsp vanilla extract

1 tsp ground cinnamon

Directions

1. Preheat oven to 350°F. Lightly butter a large and deep rectangular baking pan. I like to take the paper wrapping from butter sticks and wipe the inside of the pan with it. Make sure to work into all corners and walls.

2. Start preparing the batter by melting chocolate chips and butter in double boiler. In the meantime, beat eggs with vanilla. Also, mix all dry ingredients in large mixing bowl.

3. Once chocolate and butter are melted, remove from heat and incorporate eggs and vanilla by beating well with electric hand mixer.

4. Add wet ingredients to dry ingredients and mix well with electric hand mixer. You want a very smooth texture with no clumps.

5. Pour into your baking pan evenly. Set aside.

6. To prepare cream cheese filling, mix cream cheese, butter, and eggs until soft and smooth.

7. Add sugar, vanilla, and cinnamon; continue to mix until all is incorporated evenly.

8. Pour cream cheese filling evenly over batter in your baking pan. With a butter knife, make vertical lines from top to bottom to marry the two mixtures together.

9. Bake at 350°F for 20 minutes. Rotate pan in oven and bake another 15 minutes or until toothpick test returns clean.

10. Remove and let cool. Enjoy!

Key Lime Pie

We have a really good key lime pie at Paulie's, and they are personal sized so you can eat the whole thing! We use five-inch mini aluminum tins at the restaurant, but this recipe will work for a full size twelve-inch pie tin.

» *Measurements are by weight.*

Ingredients

4 oz graham cracker crumbs

1 oz granulated sugar

2 oz unsalted butter, melted

For Key Lime Filling

14 oz sweetened condensed milk

4 egg yolks

4 oz key lime juice

Directions

1. Mix graham cracker crumbs and sugar together. Pour in melted butter and mix thoroughly. By hand, press the crust mixture into your pie shells and chill.

2. Preheat oven to 325°F.

3. Mix together condensed milk and eggs until completely combined.

4. Add key lime juice in slow stream. When all is added, mix until completely smooth.

5. Pour into your chilled shell and bake at 325°F for 10 minutes. Filling will become firm after baking.

▶ Dipping the peanut butter cookies in chocolate makes them a bit more special.

Peanut Butter Cookies

What is the best peanut butter pairing? Chocolate! That's why we dip half of the cookie into a beautiful glossy Swiss chocolate.

» *Makes two dozen. Measurements are by weight.*

Ingredients

44 oz creamy peanut butter

18 oz Crisco shortening

30 oz light brown sugar

1 tbsp vanilla extract

4 oz milk

3 eggs

30 oz Bob's Red Mill
all-purpose flour

1 tsp salt

1 tsp baking soda

Directions

1. Preheat oven to 325°F. Lightly grease baking pan or cover with parchment paper.

2. In large mixing bowl, combine peanut butter, Crisco, brown sugar, milk, and vanilla. Beat well until blended.

3. Add eggs and beat until fully incorporated.

4. In separate bowl, mix together flour, salt, and baking soda.

5. Add flour mixture to peanut butter mixture and mix on low until all is blended evenly.

6. Form golf-ball-sized balls and place about 2 inches apart on baking sheet. With a dinner fork dipped in flour, press tines into dough ball on all 4 sides until slightly flattened.

7. Bake at 325°F for about 15 minutes, or until lightly browned around the edges. Remove and let cool.

8. If you would like to dip in chocolate, you don't have to use an expensive Swiss product. Try melting semisweet chocolate chips with a bit of butter in a double boiler. Make sure to use a bowl deep enough to cover half of the cookie when dipping. Lightly shake off any excess chocolate before returning to parchment paper. Let dry and enjoy!

After five years as chef, general manager, and operator, I started to run out of gas a bit. I was physically and emotionally exhausted.

The major reason I was doing everything myself was financial; I wasn't convinced we could afford salaried managers yet. We already had twenty-five employees, in addition to my parents, on payroll. But I had to delegate at least the front-of-house responsibilities to someone else; I could still run the back of house.

About this time, Paulie's was getting positive press, and we were seeing higher sales numbers consistently, so it was time to promote current staff members to management. I was using my public relations and marketing experience to act as the public relations department. I wrote my own press releases for Paulie's and later for Camerata (future wine bar opened in 2013). After our first year and a half at Camerata, I hired a public relations company to take some of the load off my shoulders. It's also uncomfortable writing press releases about yourself.

I also created a beverage director position to create and maintain our beer and wine list. At Paulie's, we curate an all-Italian wine list and an eclectic beer list—some local craft beer, some imports, but all delicious. Improving our beer and wine list also contributed to higher sales figures, which virtually pays for the position of the beverage director.

At Paulie's, we have two registers that customers can order from. Most days, we have to shut down one line so that we can manage the wait times on food coming out of the kitchen. Like I mentioned earlier, our kitchen is not set up great for speed, and overloading the kitchen with more tickets than it can handle will only create longer wait times. We also have a small dining room and frequently run out of tables, so slowing down the line also allows more time for tables to become available. Paulie's was never meant to be this busy, so we have to do our best to manage our guests' expectations. I would rather you wait in line a bit longer than put in your order quickly and make you wait an hour for your food or receive your food with nowhere to sit.

Cooking is the easy part in a restaurant, and that's why restaurants open—to serve food. It's the other intricacies that consume more time than anyone expects. People are the most satisfying aspect and can also be the most disappointing. I have seen many of my staff grow into well-rounded individuals and excel beyond my expectations, and I have seen some past staff not get on board. It is rewarding to see some buy in and develop further, and it can be disappointing to watch those who you've invested time in jump ship. But this job is not for everyone. Hell, this *industry* is not for everyone.

I have been blessed with a very loyal kitchen staff, and I try to earn that loyalty. One time, I received a morning phone call that one of my strongest cooks had been arrested. It didn't make much sense to me since he was not someone who usually looked for trouble. He was in the wrong place, at the wrong time, with the wrong people, and although I knew he didn't commit a crime, he knew he should not have put himself in such a questionable situation. Our kitchen cannot run without all cooks on hand, so I stepped in and worked his shifts until we could get it figured out. I could've hired someone to replace him, but it was worthwhile to me to work for him and wait for his return. He was too strong a cook and too good a person.

While he was out, another cook gave her notice, so now I had two cooks out. I did find someone to replace her, but he still needed training, so I was training the new cook on one station while filling in at the other.

This line cook job is hard; you have to be sharp. If you aren't used to it, it's easy to become rusty and to get frustrated. One day, all of the stress got to me—two cooks out, unsure when or if one would return, the new one not ready to work alone, not to mention the other responsibilities of the restaurant. I walked into my office calmly, then unloaded with a kick to a box that I thought was empty. I kicked it hard, but the box didn't budge. It took a few seconds for the pain to register in my brain, and I knew something in my foot was broken. It turns out that the box was full of printer paper.

▲ Although Paulie's is counter service, our front-of-house staff give the best customer service around.

The pain was excruciating, but I had to keep working. It's one thing to be one cook short, but one short plus a trainee could easily become a disaster. The kitchen would fall so far behind that customers would never get their food on time, creating an anxious atmosphere in the dining room. So I hobbled back to the line for dinner, telling no one what had just happened.

We got crushed, of course, and so did I. Every step was painful, but I had to keep going. The restaurant's reputation depended on me, and so did the loyalty and trust of the kitchen. This went on for days. Every night, I iced and elevated my foot, and little by little, the swelling went down. But I still had to get up and work on my feet every day.

After a month, we finally got word that my cook would be released if I could get bail money, so I hobbled up to the court, waited in line to pay the bail, and waited for my cook. I picked him up and took him home. He was so grateful to be out and to still have his job that he has worked his butt off for me. He repaid every dollar of the bail money, and he has become one of my strongest and most loyal cooks.

> ❝We got crushed, of course, and so did I. Every step was painful, but I had to keep going.❞

Taking care of my staff makes them want to take care of me and the restaurant. We all look out for each other. And my toe never healed properly, but it was worth it.

Paulie's is indeed a family-built restaurant. We are small, dependent on each other, and I open the floor for improvement suggestions from my staff. But there are also learned corporate ideals that have helped us stay consistent. One of our tenured staff, Rebecca Qian, has put together several training manuals and checklists to help new staff get on board quickly without my having to watch their every move. I had always aspired to have detailed training materials for the future, but the thought of compiling these on top of current responsibilities made me want to bury my head in the sand. My employee interviewing process paid off with Rebecca. She wasn't just an employee; she bought in. These types of employees are what make businesses run. Owners cannot possibly do everything. Early on, I thought I was a great operator because I knew how to do everything and most times would try to do everything. Now I recognize a good operator by how well his or her business runs when they are *not* there.

Besides a rare shift on the line to cover for someone, I wasn't cooking much anymore by this point. Could it be this restaurant was actually running on its own at a level I was happy with? What would I do with my free time? Could I actually have a personal life again? The answer was simple: I opened another business.

▲ Staff training is essential at Paulie's. It allows staff to teach and learn from each other, enabling future leaders.

◀ Behind-the-scenes dough making in the studio.

66 These types of employees are what make businesses run."

CHAPTER 6

Opening Camerata

Although Paulie's was running on all cylinders, I wanted to build a bit more financial security. The building that houses Paulie's has also housed other small businesses through the years. We are actually part of a 1950s strip center, although that may not be obvious from the building's exterior. The space adjacent to Paulie's has been occupied by a furniture store, a clothing store, and a women's boutique. In 2013, it became available once again, and people—mainly our customers—had been pushing me to expand the dining room space. But I knew if I expanded our seating, our tiny kitchen couldn't keep up with the extra demand in a timely manner, possibly creating customers that were more frustrated than satisfied.

I had brainstormed before on what I could do with the space if it was ever available again. One idea was an Italian retail market. I did a lot of research and number-crunching and realized that the retail game wasn't something I wanted to get into at that point. I went so far as to interview Italian-born locals to see what they'd want in a shop and as possible staff; I wanted complete authenticity. I would need a lot of imported goods, which would come at a hefty price, thus creating a very small markup if I wanted to stay affordable to our customer base. Retail markup is usually significantly less than restaurant markup, and with restaurant profit margins already razor thin, this didn't sound like a feasible business plan.

After realizing a market wasn't the best model for me, I considered an intimate wine bar. Beer and wine markups are higher than retail, which leaves more room for error. It meant the bar didn't have to be busy all the time to survive. We could still have a quiet and relaxed atmosphere while still making enough profit for longevity.

I wanted to flip the switch, to create a more mature room at Paulie's, similar to a dual concept. Paulie's is very casual and family friendly, but I wanted the wine bar to be a quiet, intimate space to relax that initiated more intelligent conversation. I also thought that if the wine bar took off, it would introduce Paulie's to a more cultivated clientele, thus increasing the longevity of the business as a whole.

▶ GM Chris Poldoian
is always working.

▲ Preopening of Camerata—quite messy.

> **66** Camerata is the best thing I have done to date."

Initially, I wanted the bar to be a true speakeasy. I was planning to change the entry password weekly and to update patrons through an approved email list. I also thought of blacking out the front windows and locking the front doors, having access only through the back door in the parking lot. The interior would be dark, sexy, and very comfortable. Paulie's has a beer and wine license, so we were already set.

After much thought and planning, I decided I wanted to go the opposite direction from secrecy, to become warm and welcoming. Wine can be an intimidating subject, and I was afraid the speakeasy would come across as pretentious. The space is adjacent to Paulie's (they literally share a wall), so we could bust through and add a doorway that connects the two spaces, expanding the square footage of the current business.

Camerata has an aesthetic and atmosphere completely different from that of Paulie's. Camerata is urban and chic, yet pleasing and comfortable. Our designer, Gin Braverman, did a fantastic job of

▶ The staff at Camerata is incredibly gracious and helpful.

▼ Camerata has a modern industrial look that translates to warm and welcoming.

▼ Camerata often hosts wine tastings, wine-maker events, and buyouts.

◀ Although the bar is only 1,500 square feet, the layout allows for plenty of seating.

combining concrete and grays to create a neutral environment so that the wine could be the focus, but her layout of bar and bench seating on top of perfect lighting allowed for an intimate setting.

Camerata was built on a shoestring budget, which Paulie's funded itself (remember the savings account I mentioned earlier?). All of our opening employees had a hand in building and cleaning the bar before opening day. I wanted the staff to take ownership and care about the status of the bar, and I wanted them to see how small businesses are opened.

Camerata is the best thing I have done to date. It has helped bring a new customer base into the restaurant and has added to the potential longevity of the Paulie's–Camerata compound.

The name was taken from the Florentine Camerata, a group of artists, musicians, intellectuals, and writers in Renaissance Florence. The term literally means a "room" or "chamber" where gatherings are held. The Florentine Camerata incubated some of the greatest art and music in the history of Florence. The name rings true because of my Italian heritage, my appreciation for music and art, as well as my desire to cultivate excellence in that space.

Camerata's platform would be built around education. I wanted to inform the customer, not intimidate them. Wine is already an overwhelming subject to the novice, so I wanted to remove that shadow and open up the conversation, spreading accurate information to a larger, wine-supporting community. We do that through a well-trained staff and dedication to professional service.

Camerata has been very well received in the Montrose District of Houston. I am proud to have brought such an important and large space (1,500 square feet!) to the Houston wine community. Camerata appeared on several "Best Wine Bar" lists during our first few months of opening. After our first year, we got the attention of national publications as well.

The next accomplishment would be recognition for Camerata's wine program from the James Beard Foundation; unfortunately, a wine program must be in existence for five years before being considered, so we'll be working hard awaiting 2019. We're often approached by developers who want to expand Camerata to other locations in Houston. At this point, I am not sure that is the right move for this particular concept, but I would not be opposed to sharing Camerata's vision in other cities. We'll have to wait to see what happens.

Paulie's

EST. '98

CHAPTER 7

The Future of Paulie's

Business has been good for Paulie's overall ever since our first year, which is a blessing in itself. But around 2013, we started to see an increase in positive press. This was about the time all the insane hard work started to meld together. My family's vision was becoming a reality. Not all staff could see the vision in my head, but they believed in me and supported me through all the changes.

The years of working on the line next to my cooks, the countless interviews trying to find strong staff, and the work ethic I instilled in myself so that it would spread throughout the business were finally paying off. The kitchen was pumping on all cylinders, and the front-of-house staff was growing more professional. Paulie's was consistently making "best of" lists and being mentioned in local press, including *Houston Press*, Zagat, *Houston Chronicle*, *Houston Business Journal*, CultureMap, *My Table*, Eater, and a few national publications like *Maxim*.

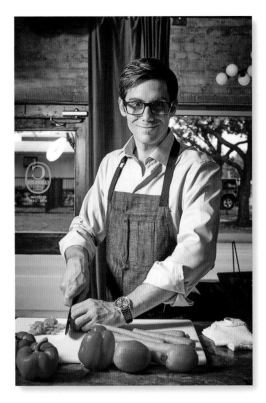

▲ Sample photo from Tiffany and Co. watch shoot. I don't usually prep vegetables at the bar. . . .

In 2015, Tiffany & Co. approached me about endorsing their new line of men's watches. I was honored and agreed. I believe the only other chef at the time endorsing Tiffany & Co. was Marcus Samuelsson, a celebrated chef in New York known not only for his amazing food but also for his sense of style.

I was initially concerned about the Tiffany endorsement. Paulie's has always been a family-run neighborhood restaurant, and no matter the success, I always wanted it to stay that way. I was afraid what it would say about me by accepting a partnership with a global brand like Tiffany & Co. I considered turning it down. Then they proposed holding the launch party at Camerata. I felt like Camerata could use the exposure, and a brand like Tiffany & Co made more sense with the global reach of our wine selections, so I went for it.

The satisfaction and fulfillment I slowly began to feel as I saw all these things come into fruition was overwhelming. I felt like I'd had my head down, working, for years, and once I lifted it up to see, there were smiling faces all around.

After putting all my eggs into the Paulie's basket, not knowing truly if it would succeed had been gut wrenching. It's always important to keep your staff motivated; that's what keeps the wheels turning. But who motivates the owner? I didn't have a supervisor or mentor that was pushing me. I had to find that in myself somehow and consistently. It was a struggle, but we made it together.

The positive press and increase in consistent sales set us up for increased longevity. Some people may not understand that restaurants often need positive press to stay relevant and to project future sales. We don't really like being public figures—at least, I don't. I'm quiet, and I want my work to speak for itself. But I do realize how important it is to network and to make myself available for interviews. I try to share my views on issues that affect restaurants and restaurant employees and hope that something good will come of it. The increased sales allowed me to continuously promote our employees, giving out raises and benefits. I haven't given myself a raise since 2012, but our success has allowed me to take time to actually rest my mind and body. I've traveled more, watched more movies, and started working out again. I slowly overcame the anxiety and stress and built a better me. I noticed myself becoming more patient and less hasty with decisions. I let my staff start making decisions on their own, and I was okay with them making mistakes, as long as they learned from them. I never imagined things would go this well.

I am humbled and grateful for all the customers and staff that stuck with Paulie's. We had good years, and we had transitional years, and there are so many faces that stuck with us through it all; it's pretty damn amazing.

One very special lady named Suzanne has been coming to Paulie's since we first opened in 1998. She arrives sharply at 11:00 a.m., just as we open, and sits at the same table every time. She orders only about three different things on the menu; our regular customers seem to always know what they want.

Another old friend of Paulie's is a gentleman named Charles, who was a well-known architect in Houston. Charles was just wrapping up his career and heading into retirement when we got to know him. He was like a celebrity when he walked in. Not only did our staff know him, but he always had friends around the restaurant. Charles passed away in 2015, and we miss him. Your customers become so familiar that they feel like family. Seeing Charles's last few years was like watching a grandparent age and pass on, but I'm grateful for his time with us.

Paulie's has many special family members like Charles and Suzanne.

> 66 The positive press and increase in consistent sales set us up for increased longevity."

I have always believed in giving back to the community, and I am always happy to open my doors during off days to support a needy cause. In addition to pop-ups held to raise money, Paulie's often donates gift cards and food to local schools and churches. But above all, I think the most philanthropic thing I've done is assisting in opening Houston's only charity bar, OKRA Charity Saloon. At OKRA, we give away 100 percent of our profits. We select four different charities each month to compete for the winnings. Patrons are encouraged to vote for their favorite charity through drink tickets, and the charity with the most votes at the end of the month wins.

OKRA was opened in December 2012, and we have given away about $200,000 each year. By the time this book is published, we will have surpassed $1 million donated to Houston charities.

I was designated the kitchen manager when we opened, so I came up with a simple bar menu that included panini, salad, beef jerky, different waffle fries, and baked-to-order chocolate chip cookies. I also spent every night in the bar our first month, training the kitchen staff. Since then, I have served as vice president and secretary of the organization. I am very proud of my association with this little bar.

LIST OF REGULARS

Suzanne, Dorothy, and Taylor

Tim and Joe

Ashley Preston

Roger Moore

Doug and Bunny

Frank

Dana and James

Carl Nicchio

Gina and Hyder

W. L. and Lynn Gray

Leonard and Cheryl Burrow

Tommie and Pamela Rape

Chad

Rolland and Sherry St. Aubin

Larry

Debbie and Jeremiah

Robert Jobe

Eric Sandler

Greenway Coffee family

Andrew Edmonson

Philip

Esther and Mel

Georgeos Kazilas

Robert and Kay Baily

Richard Herman

Linda Salinas

Matt Tabor and Leslie Slade

Cathy Foreman

Nancy Tennant

Mr. Salls

Bettie

Kathy and Stuart Dissen

Elizabeth Young

Graden

Elenor

Michael Fulmer

Mr. Greenman

Don

Ray

Herb and Margerie

Carol and Herman

Mark

J. D. and Annie

Bill Kelly

Gary

Rebekah Gonzo

Dan Braun

Katie, Bob, and Joseph

Lee Collins

Olive E. Guthrei

Terry Williams

Bobby Huegel

Liz Fenton

Richard and Karen Petty

Calvin Morgan

Bob Stout

Robert and Mary Barrett

Sarah and Joe

John Spadaro

Jazmin and Lourdes Lee

Elouise

Chris Shepherd and
Lindsey Brown

Jody Stevens

Mark Salvie

Eleni Ntounakis

Timothy A. Pikey

Alvin Schultz

Donald Sampley

Jim Ewing

Andrew Edmonson

Staff at Da Marco's

Staff at Camerata

Justin Vann

Brad Hensler

Justin Burrow

Pam and Wes Lee

John Peterson and Jenny Vo

Marie Flanigan Interiors staff

Sojourn church members

Jillian Bartolome and
Drew Gimma

Doug Sheridan

Jeff Peña and Aimee Phillips

The Huynh Family

The Hinkle family

Michael Benestante

Sarah, Jim, Kevin Holmes,
and Pat Chica

Patrick Kilkeney

Annie Tindell

Anna Domning

Julia and John Stallcup

Lisa and Sydney Ellis

Southland Hardware

John J. Antel

London Ham

Kathrin Schaaf and family

Dorian Gray and family

Charlie Walne

Taste of Texas

Eluoise Charles

Julia Williams and family

Josh and Chandler Busby

Kale Petersen

Taylor Byrne Dodge

Anvil staff, past and present

Vincent Huynh

Amelie and Forrest deSpain

Justin Yu

Nicole Cruz

Stephen Maislin

Charles Tapley

Vicky and Mason

Kris, Liz, Frank, and George Cox

Kevin and Sarah Cox

Jake, Jamie, Lily, and Levi Toner

Paul and Tina Sonderfan

Brett, Patricia, Fiona, and
Bennett Boland

Jay, Joanna, and Dean Frazier

Randy Ho

Brad Gilde

Danny and Laura

Mike and Mo

Siegel-Gardner family

Lainey Collum

Alba Huerta

Russell Brightwell

AND MANY, MANY MORE . . .

▶ Some of the most talented and gracious people in the city!

▶ I am very proud of being involved with OKRA Charity Bar. It has touched the city of Houston in more ways than I imagined.

By the time this book is published, we will have surpassed $1 million donated to Houston charities."

Beef Jerky

When we opened OKRA Charity Bar, I was given the role of kitchen manager, which meant creating a bar food menu and training staff to execute. The key to a consistent menu without my daily presence is simplicity. Try to remove as much guesswork as possible. This jerky recipe is really tasty and easy to follow. You will need a food dehydrator. This is a batch recipe, but it's jerky, so seal it and save it!

Ingredients

- 10 lb lean flank steak, sliced thin, across the grain
- 3 cups Worcestershire sauce
- 3 cups soy sauce
- 8 tsp fresh ground black pepper
- 8 tsp onion powder
- 4 tsp red pepper flakes

Directions

1. Trim any fat from meat before slicing. Slice *across* the grain into slender pieces. Slicing across the grain will make it easier to tear when eating.

2. Combine all the ingredients in mixing bowl and mix well, add meat, and toss well. Make sure meat is submerged; you can add a bit more Worcestershire and soy sauce depending on your storage bin. Cover in plastic and refrigerate overnight.

3. Lay meat on trays to dry, and pat dry with paper towels, trying to remove any excess liquid.

4. Set dehydrator to 145°F. Dry for approximately 4 hours. It is ready when dark yet pliable. You don't want any red meat showing.

5. Eat right away or store airtight in refrigerator.

Chocolate Chip Cookies

These cookies can be found at Paulie's daily and also at OKRA Charity Bar in downtown Houston. At OKRA, we bake to order, which means they come straight from the oven to you, with a side of cold milk!

» *Makes two dozen. Measurements are by weight.*

Ingredients

1 lb Bob's Red Mill all-purpose flour

1 tsp baking soda

1 tsp salt

12 oz unsalted butter, room temp

12 oz light brown sugar

6 oz granulated sugar

1 tsp vanilla extract

3 eggs

18 oz semisweet chocolate chips

6 oz chopped walnuts

Directions

1. Preheat oven to 325°F. Grease baking sheet or cover in parchment paper.

2. Mix together butter, eggs, vanilla, and both sugars until well blended.

3. In another bowl, combine flour, salt, and baking soda.

4. Add butter mixture to flour mixture and beat with electric hand mixer until blended. Stir in chocolate chips and walnuts.

5. Form golf-ball-size balls and place 3 inches apart on baking sheet. Bake 15 minutes or until light brown. Remove and let cool. Enjoy with cold milk!

Since its inception in 1998, Paulie's has fed millions of mouths, created jobs for hundreds of people, and given back thousands of dollars to the community. Paulie's will never receive a James Beard award; our biggest accomplishment, to me, is operating consistently for twenty years. We survived a national financial crisis, numerous floods, Hurricane Rita, Hurricane Harvey, countless break-ins, and a gluten-free epidemic. I hope that Paulie's thrives for as long as I am alive, and I hope our city and community continue to support us. At Paulie's, we plan to continue to give the city consistent and delicious food.

Thank you for being part of the family.

Index

Rigatoni Bolognese, 47
T-Bone Fiorentina, 81, *85*
Veal Saltimbocca, 19
Messina, Sicily, 100
Mia's, 7
Milan, Italy, 92
Mosbacher, Kathi, 69
Mushroom Risotto, 33
mushrooms
 Grilled Portobello
  Sandwich, 65
 Mushroom Risotto, 33
Mussels, Fettuccini with, 79

N

Naples, Italy, 100
Neapolitan Margherita Pizza,
 102–3
Ninfa's, 7, 58
Nino's, 7

O

OKRA Charity Saloon, 138,
 171, *176–77, 178–81, 186*
Onion, Pickled, 13
Oxheart, 126
 see also Justin Yu, 126
 see also Willet Feng, 126

P

Palermo, Sicily, 100–101
panini, *101*
Pappas Restaurant Group, 126
 see also Justin Basye, 126

see also Michael Gaspard,
 126
The Pass & Provisions, *see also*
 Seth Siegel-Gardner, 47
pasta
 Black Pasta Dough, 137
 Cacio e Pepe, 114
 Creste di Gallo with
  Marinara and Sausage, 13
 Egg Pasta Dough, 137
 Fettuccini Alfredo, 39
 Fettuccini Scampi, 9
 Fettuccini with Mussels, 79
 Fusilli Pesto, 44
 Lobster Ravioli, *14–15,*
  16–17
 Pasta con Sarde, *52–53,* 54
 Paulie's method, 135–38
 Puttanesca, 20
 Rigatoni Bolognese, 47
 Spaghetti Caesar, 23
 Spaghetti Nero, 98
 Tortellini in Brodo, 106–7
Paulie's. *See also* Camerata
 beers and wines, 148
 coffee program, 128–35
 customer service, 85, 88, 128,
  148
 desserts, 138
 employees, 67–69, 82, 84–85,
  148–49, 155, *174–75*
 family influences, 57–58, 67,
  68–69, 82, 85, 88
 future of, 169–71, 182

 history of, 57–58, 67–69, 82,
  84–85, 88, 169–71, 182
 Holcombe location, 92, 101,
  110
 management of, 110, 148–49
 operating costs, 67–69
 order volume, 69, 82–85,
  148–49
 pasta-making at, 135–38
 pop-ups at, 125–26
 press coverage about, 69,
  126, 148, 169–70
 recipe sources, 1 (*See also*
  individual recipes)
 regular customers, 171,
  172–73
 restaurant industry and,
  67–68, 148
 Westheimer location, 85,
  125–28, 135–38
Paulie's Caesar Dressing, 24
Paulie's Marinara, 10
Paulie's Vinaigrette, 72
Peanut Butter Cookies, *144–45,*
 147
Pears, Roasted, *111,* 122
Pesto, 44
Petronella, Bernard, 3, 6, 57–58,
 68–69
Petronella, Frank Paul, 6, 85, 88
Petronella, Kathy, 6, 57–58,
 61–65, *69,* 138
Petronella, Paul
 advertising career, 91–92

▲ Our first OKRA fundraiser held at Paulie's AKA
"Moneycat" brunch. Pictured is Chris Shepherd and
Seth Siegel-Gardner.

About the Author

Paul Petronella is the namesake and operator of his family's restaurant, Paulie's (pauliesrestaurant.com), where he has dedicated his life to help make Paulie's the best it can be to its guests and staff. He is a noted restaurateur, cook, and philanthropist with a lifetime of experience in independent restaurant life.

In 2015, Houston Press named Paulie's "Best Montrose Neighborhood Restaurant." Petronella was added to the *Houston Chronicle*'s "Most Interesting Men," a listing of Houston's most influential men, including entrepreneurs, philanthropists, and professional athletes. Tiffany and Co. also named him a Houston influencer for their new CT60 Watch Collection.

Paul is passionate about the food and beverage industry in Houston and how it affects the lives of guests and restaurant workers. Through multiple leadership roles at OKRA Charity Saloon, he has helped fund and launch charitable programs throughout the city of Houston by donating over $1 million—and counting—to sixty different local charitable organizations.

Paul has a BBA from Texas State University and received his MBA through onsite restaurant life. He's an AAU youth basketball coach and lives in Houston's Heights community.